Detoxing the Perfect Family

Chris Volkmann
Toren Volkmann

ELTON-WOLF PUBLISHING

WHAT READERS SAY

I applaud your effort to produce a book which is at least partially based upon your experience and your intense interest in helping families cope with the reality of alcohol in our culture and in the lives of our young people.

(Rev.) Edward A. Malloy, C.S.C.
President, University of Notre Dame
CASA Board Member,
National Center on Addiction & Substance Abuse

This book is a treasure of education, insight and experience about alcoholism. The authors have captured the essence of the struggle millions of families go through to get out of the alcoholic system and into recovery. Reading this book will open your brain, your guts and your heart to an effective way of processing this diabolical disease.

C.J. Kirk, LICSW
Senior Alcohol and Drug Consultant to Peace Corps
Office of Medical Services (1984-2004)

Having been involved in adolescent chemical dependency treatment for over twenty-eight years, I think *Our Drink* is a profoundly honest and real story that all families could benefit from. The back and forth dialogue between parent and child about the pain, fear, and destructive consequences makes it feel like you have witnessed a ten-round boxing match.

I can see this book being used by prevention folks working with high school students, college-age students and their parents, school, and staff. It could also be used in treatment. I found everything in this book well done.

Our Drink brings the reality home that alcohol does not care who it conquers, and that the more sophisticated we think we are, the more the destruction surprises and hurts those who are captured by its power. It becomes very clear in this fearless searching diary, that being perfect is painful, and that the condition is a myth with consequences.

Stephen Bogan, M.A., Chemical Dependency Professional
Division of Substance Abuse, State of Washington
Nationally Certified Addiction Counselor, Youth Treatment Lead

The strongest argument of *Our Drink* is that alcoholism sucks. *One of my main* concerns is how to get *Our Drink* to people BEFORE alcoholism has taken over. It's necessary that this book be read by both parents and kids and discussed before the issue arises!

Sean Walsh, age 24
University of California San Diego
Graduate Engineering student

Other people need to read this! Particularly, I thought of our group of friends, and how many (if not all) of us could stand to reevaluate the role of drinking in our lives. Then, I thought that my mother and others in families similar to mine would want to read it. Reading *Our Drink* has inspired me to do some much-needed introspection about my own habits and attitudes regarding alcohol use/abuse.

Chris Maxwell, age 21
Recent college graduate, Boston University

Because college is such a life-changing experience and drinking such a big part of it, *Our Drink* will have an impact on campuses everywhere. I learned a lot, I cried, and the honesty was touching.

Susan Fiksdal, Ph.D.
The Evergreen State College

Our Drink delves into the mircro-levels of alcoholism. This is a great resource for families trying to weed out addiction issues and provides an amazing example of a family working together to make all members succeed.

We're always taught to pay attention in school; to go to college and get that great job; to find a soul mate, house, car, kids and all that stuff we "need." As soon as we question whether we need it we feel like we've been wrong. Maybe this is what drives us to drink. Maybe we're just a bunch of wimps who have nothing better to do than wait around until our "problem genes" catch a whiff of the wrong substance and send us spiraling downhill. It's incredible all of us aren't addicted to something. *Our Drink* lays it all out.

Despite the lament over what went wrong, Toren and Chris Volkmann have taken a terrible situation and created something beautiful that I think will help others. Toren's story is so important because it isn't the story you always hear. Several of my friends are definitely part of the one-third college kids with alcohol issues. We are all supposedly the "perfect kids" from "perfect families" yet still keep boozing. This book speaks to us and our families. Awesome!

Dan Murphy, age 24
Recent college grad, Lewis & Clark College

Our Drink made me look at my own life and my addiction of twenty years: smoking. I quit! Thank you, Perfect Family!!!

Anonymous reader

Our Drink is right on because it allows us to see addiction from both the addict and the parent. There aren't many books written in this style. Families, particularly parents, will find this book a helpful tool to understand addiction. I recommend using this book in programs that are geared towards adolescents.

Our Drink will make a profound impact on education of the disease concept. This book will help move our society towards acceptance, which in turn will open doors for higher quality treatment and decrease the tendency to look at the disease as a "moral issue." I will definitely recommend this book to my patients!

Katie Revenaugh, BS, CDP
Chemical Dependency Professional

Learning about drinking choices early on and being proactive can prevent horrific tragedies and loss of life. There are so many parents who will relate to *Our Drink*.

Patty Layton
City of Olympia, WA
Safe & Sober Driving Coordinator

Our Drink helped me understand a reserved student I was wondering about. He's in trouble academically. After reading the book, I told my student to be honest with his parents; that they want to know him *and* his struggles. He really appreciated that.

Anonymous college professor

Our Drink made me look at myself and my friends. And we're the target audience! Well...maybe our moms, too. A wonderful blend of introspection, narration, and valuable information!

Anonymous College Student

. . .ABOUT ALCOHOL AND BINGE DRINKING:

The reason 1400 kids die each year is because they weren't taught how to consume alcohol in moderation.

Isaac Thorn, age 23
University of Cincinnati, in *USA Today*

That college students drink to get drunk is no myth. It is the simple truth.

Philip Meyer, Professor of Journalism,
University of North Carolina, Chapel Hill, in *USA Today*

Stanford recently banned alcohol in public spaces of freshman dorms. But that just pushes froshes into private rooms to drink.

Joey Naoli, 21
Stanford University, in *USA Today*

Alcohol is the most serious public health problem on American college campuses today.

David Satcher
U.S. Surgeon General

In the past we thought of alcohol as a more benign drug. It's not included in the war on drugs...[But] the most popular drug is also an incredibly dangerous drug.

Sandra Brown, researcher
University of California, San Diego, in *Dying to Drink*

As a national goal, the U.S. Surgeon General has established a 50% reduction in college binge drinking by the year 2010.

Our Drink

Detoxing the Perfect Family

Our Drink
www.ourdrink.com

Front cover image and type by Zetein
Back cover image by Toren Volkmann

Cover design by Beth Farrell
Text design by Colleen Edwards

Published by Elton-Wolf Publishing
Seattle, Washington

The names and locations of some of the people described in this book have been changed to protect privacy. Reference information for Internet and addresses were accurate at the time of publication. Resources provided are a compilation and not necessarily endorsed by the authors.

ISBN: 1-58619-106-3
Library of Congress Card Catalogue Number: 2004108720

First Printing August 2004
Printed in Canada

ELTON-WOLF PUBLISHING

2505 Second Avenue Suite 515   Seattle, Washington 98121
Tel 206.748.0345 Fax 206.748.0343
www.elton-wolf.com info@elton-wolf.com

To my family and friends
- TV

To Don—parent, husband, advocate
- CV

ACKNOWLEDGMENTS

For vision and critical acumen alongside her steadfast loyalty, we thank Susan Fiksdal.

Sincere appreciation to our first readers whose suggestions and insights shaped our work and focused our energy: Mike Boyd, Patty Layton, Joan Marchioro, Chris Maxwell, Dan Murphy, Sean Walsh.

Our heartfelt gratitude extends to staff and volunteers of the Peace Corps for their professional response and remarkable understanding. C.J. Kirk, thank you for direction and validation. To Larry Perez at University of San Diego, thanks for your guidance and persistence. We would like to acknowledge Toren's sponsor, Matt.

For believing in our project, thank you to Beth Farrell at Elton-Wolf. Hal Scogin and his staff at Zetein poured themselves into our website, **www.ourdrink.com**; we appreciate their dedication.

This book is inspired in remembrance of Ric Volkmann, Montana Donini, and Nadia Melinkovich. Their struggles have become a part of us.

We are bolstered by the encouragement of our extended family and cadre of loyal friends, you who inspired us to honestly face ourselves and then write it all down.

Special recognition to Tanler Volkmann and Tyson Volkmann for their support and compassion—for being perfect brothers.

And finally, thank you especially to Don Volkmann for his patience, humor and endless love.

Contents

1

A PERFECT START

FRIENDS AND ACQUAINTANCES JOKED ABOUT OUR FAMILY, HOW THEY couldn't stand us: the successful suburban medical family with three "knock-'em-dead" boys—athletic, smart, charismatic hunks with a strong work ethic and sensitivity; my husband with killer abs and two medical specialty degrees; and me, the mom who was a Renaissance woman, an ex-classroom teacher having abandoned the public schools to lead her family to the pinnacle of fulfillment. Yup. Our family did it all: kids turning out for three varsity sports each year, music lessons, community volunteering, snow skiing, the right parties, the right clothes, the right colleges, the right summer jobs, the right family events. Our boys had supportive grandparents and aunts and uncles; dinner together in the family home; household chores, mowing the lawn; and a pet beagle—a true nuclear family myth.

All our golden boys graduated from college, and successfully: the three blond brothers. We could breathe a sigh of relief. We could stick out our chests, sound our horn and proclaim that, indeed, our way of raising kids was the greatest. We had done it the right way. Mom, forsaking her career and founding a public school art docent volunteer program while running marathons and playing viola in the local symphony, proved that this was the altruistic spirit needed to form a better America; Dr. Dad, coaching soccer and coordinating team sports efforts between on-call jags, epitomized devotion.

Backpacking throughout the Northwest as a family built the

1

boys' character and persistence. They seemed to temper rebelliousness by a perfect balance of good manners and positive intent. For successfully raising children, high school honors societies and college boards of trustees everywhere could look to our family for the manual on "how to do it."

Did we dwell on the bumps in the road? As little as possible. Did we hang out the dirty laundry? Seldom. Kids will be kids after all. And boys! What a challenge! Those energetic rascals! Not to mention their parents who also lived adventuresome lives; not all parents leave the country to trek in Northern India the same day war begins in Afghanistan. We certainly showed our kids how to live on the edge!

Well, to be honest, our family did have its ups and downs. The boys gave us our share of sleepless nights. They were naughty on the playground in grade school, acted out in a class or two, and in high school, slipped out at night and experimented with alcohol and drugs. In fact, if you added up infractions over the years, we had a ledgerful. There were imposed penalties and restrictions, along with some MIPs. ('Minor in Possession' is the charge for underage kids who drink and are caught by the law.) We intervened; we even purchased a Breathalyzer and checked the boys when they came home on their high school curfew. But most people advised us not to worry about such missteps. They were part of growing up. Everyone had them in their youth.

During college, the brothers returned home for breaks and we were concerned they partied too much. They stayed out too late. Drank too much. And we suspected that at times they had smoked and sampled other social drugs. But my husband and I tried to be understanding because we had done that same sort of thing in the 1970s. We'd handled it. And we had talked with our kids about moderation, about binge drinking, about setting goals, about not closing doors by taking thoughtless risk. We had been up front with them. Our family weathered those things, and now, we were on to better. Afterall, our kids had graduated from college. Their youthful indiscretions were history. We had successfully hatched, nurtured, and educated them for the larger world. Now we could sit back and watch them take their places.

Until that phone call.

It was the call from our 24-year-old son, the youngest, the call telling us he was considering committing himself to a rehab program for alcoholism.

Becoming an alcoholic couldn't have been that simple for our son, especially now that I look back on it. There had been clues about what might happen, *about what was happening*. But until we filled in the scattered, morphed shapes on our paint-by-number childrearing tableau, until we stepped back, we couldn't see. We were blind to the surreal family we may have, in fact, created. It was difficult for us to recognize our youngest son among the stricken slashes of color and pattern, and tough to make out his two brothers, camouflaged there as well. Then, identifying *ourselves* took even more scrutiny. Through this painful process, I realized that the story of our Perfect Family needs to be told.

The problem of our drink isn't just *too much to drink*; it is the fact that alcohol addiction happens before our very eyes, under the brazen label of success. We don't recognize it under our noses. That's what is scary. Our son was killing himself in our presence, over several years time, and we didn't see it. If we are an average family and the statistics about binge drinking in public schools and colleges are true, then there must be more families like us in the United States—in the world. That's why this book.

"When did this happen?" we asked our son. A college graduate for hardly a year at this point, Toren confessed not only to having drunk alcohol since early high school, but that he had been binge drinking since that time. He said that's where it started. And we discovered that even though our son graduated from the D.A.R.E. program (Drug Abuse Resistance Education, a drug and alcohol education program offered in the public schools) and was accepted into high school Honors Society, he had outsmarted us and even himself when it came to the deception of alcohol abuse.

Many kids these days talk casually about drinking or getting wasted, or binge drinking and blacking out. It's like mentioning going to a latte stand, as commonplace as snacking on popcorn at a ball game. Binge drinking is not only a social custom among youth, it is a social epidemic. In fact, binge drinking is the most widespread health problem in the U.S. on college campuses. The percentage of students who said they drank alcohol to get drunk climbed from 39.9 percent in 1993 to 48.2 percent in 2001.[1] Drinking to get drunk is cited as the primary reason for consuming alcohol by 47 percent of students who drink.[2] The U.S. Surgeon General has established a goal of 50 percent reduction in college binge drinking by the year 2010.[3]

After Toren's call, I searched the web, thinking I might find books talking about the problem from the viewpoint of family. There were some that discussed binging and others that presented information about alcohol and addiction, but missing was a matter-of-fact dialogue for families, one that addresses current practices of alcohol consumption in our cul-de-sacs and on our campuses.

Particularly absent was the bruised authenticity delivered by Toren when he sent us a journal entry revealing how he'd fallen from the lap of the Peace Corps while volunteering in South America. It seemed Toren had slid overnight from a position of responsibility and respect into the depths of alcoholism where he faced immediate inpatient admittance to a rehabilitation facility. But Toren's severe problem with alcohol did not originate on a Peace Corps assignment in a foreign country. It began perhaps even before he was born. It marched through his youth and we missed all the signals. It trod through his adolescence and we thought it merely a flirtation. Now this alcohol calamity threatens to shred the veneer of our Perfect Family. It has stomped on all that we provided for Toren and his brothers and kicked it in our faces.

When Toren called with the news of his alcoholism, I thought it was the end. So we'll start there—the end at the beginning.

2

The End at the Beginning

22 September 2003. When I got the call on my answering machine, I was in shock. It was in three languages: English, Guarani, and Spanish. How do you understand a message like this even in one language? Toren greeted us in Guarani, an Indian dialect of South America where he had been working for the past six months in a tiny village. "*Mba'eichepa*," he said. The greeting means, "How are you?" But I couldn't reply to a recorded message. So I stood there and replayed it, just to make sure.

"Don't worry," he went on in Spanish. And that began a month of worrying like hell, like I had never worried before. I worried about him immediately. I worried about him in the future. I worried about him in the past, about all the mistakes we'd made in our Perfect Family.

"Mom and Dad, it's Toren. *Estoy en Washington, D.C., No se preocupe.* I'll call you later. *Todo esta bien. Bueno. Chao.*" All is well. Don't worry.

Right. I'm not worrying. I don't know what's wrong, why he called. He's supposed to be in South America. Now he's suddenly in the United States, calling me in the middle of hauling groceries in from the garage. I just got home to this, the mystery message. I don't even know what I shouldn't be worrying about, *in any language*.

I imagine all the things possible: he's very ill, he got into legal trouble trying to get across a border, he contracted malaria. Do they have malaria in the Chaco of South America? I run for a map.

I look up the emergency number in the parents' Peace Corps Manual called *On the Home Front: A Handbook for the Families of Volunteers.* Its offices are in Washington, D.C., and I'm in Washington State on the other side of the country, in a time zone three hours away. It tells me not to bother them unless it's very important. This must be important, but Toren said he would call back. I shouldn't overreact. He's twenty-four. He'll call. I put the rest of the groceries away. I weed our autumn garden, ripping out tired alyssum. I want to phone someone, but whom? And the next three hours stumble by.

When he finally calls again early that evening, the first thing he tells me is that his phone card might run out any second.

"Talk," I command him.

So he does. He asks what version I want. "You see, I've been real honest here and there's stuff coming down. Or should I not tell you?"

"Tell me."

And he does. "It's alcohol."

Alcoholism. It's only alcohol, I reassure myself. Not a really serious drug like crack or heroin or cocaine. I know lots of people who don't drink. They do perfectly fine.

But then I realize all his dreams are shattered—all that effort to apply to the Peace Corps, interview, train, his preparation for grad school—all down the drain, the hours of instruction in Spanish and Guarani. Shipped home from the Peace Corps in worse shape than a housewife on OxyContin. Dethroned from his roots in the jungle of South America where he was working with people he could help, people who were supposed to be worse off than he.

"Mom," he warns me, "I'm sending you some of my writing. Stuff I wrote down in South America last May, titled, '*My Drink.*' It's pretty blunt. You'll read some things about what I did in college. How I wasted it. I'm sorry. It sounds bad. And I suppose it is. I could've worked a lot harder. But I still appreciate all you did and I know it was at least partially a good experience. I hate to have you read this, but I have to be truthful about myself." He pauses, "It's time."

I'm standing in my kitchen on our state-of-the-art slate floors leaning on honed granite to keep from falling over in shock. Solid rock is the only material capable of holding me up. The phone card could expire any second. "When did this happen?" I blurt out. "It's so sudden!"

"No, it's been happening. You'll see. I wrote about it in my journal last May. And now it's September. But I couldn't take it anymore. I realized something was very wrong. I've been having bad side effects now and recently they're really horrible. I'm afraid."

"What side effects? Tell me." I can hardly breathe. We're suddenly cutting out the garnishes and serving up a plain slab of meat. Unsalted. Bland. Cold. I can't believe I'm listening to my son who I haven't seen since January, talking to me nine months later about detoxing in the boondocks of South America.

"It's been worse and worse every time I drank. I get the shakes, I can't sleep, I'm losing my memory; I have leg cramps," he explains.

"But how did you decide to get help?" I ask. I really wanted to know more, like how often he'd been feeling that way, how much he'd drunk, what he was drinking, why he was drinking, and how this could be happening?

"I went to the capital city for interim training. All the volunteers were there. We'd had a lot of meetings, and I couldn't make it through one without the shakes. So I'd go out and buy some *caña* (local liquor) to calm myself, and I hated the feelings that were coming over me. It was getting bad."

"Oh, Toren."

"And so I went to see the nurse. Remember when you told me once about Dustin?"

I remembered. It had been one of those whispered conversations between two mothers bumping into one another a year or two after their kids had graduated from high school, after huddling along the sidelines of football games, after the worries of athletic steroids, drugs, alcohol, and all the fearsome temptations of adolescence. Dustin's mother confided in me, asking me not to tell *anyone* whatsoever. She said that they'd had to pick up Dustin from college because he was having seizures, alcohol problems. But I hadn't kept my word because, soon after, I heard my boys talking about Dustin at a party of reunited high school chums over holiday vacation, and how Dustin was out of control. So I told my boys what Dustin's mother had confided. It had scared me. And I knew they saw Dustin occasionally, had played sports with him in the past. I thought it might make an impression on them.

"Well," Toren continues, "I always remembered what you told me about Dustin. How serious it was, and I got to thinking, I'm having some of the same problems. So I confessed to Peace Corps, to get some help."

Toren had been assigned to a small village in southern South America where he lived in a whitewashed hut with a tin and straw roof and an outhouse in back. He'd formed friendships with people in his village, planted a garden, and was preparing to work with them on a mutual project. Toren adored his assignment and the South American villagers. Peace Corps allowed him the opportunity to learn languages, to interact in a new culture and, hopefully, to better others' lives. It was Toren's aspiration after college, and he had planned to use the experience as a springboard for graduate work in psychology. I pictured him in South America picking corn, digging roots for his dinner, plucking chickens.

"And what did the nurse say?" I ask him.

"She had to turn me in and a lot happened that I'll tell you later but they medivac'd me outta there. Now I'm here in D.C. getting evaluated," he says thickly.

"Are you okay?"

"Well, I had people with me for three days straight, helping me detox. They gave me Valium. It's my last day of it."

Valium, the drug of the 1960s and '70s, for my son. In some remote South American backdrop. I'm holding my breath now. I don't think I can inhale one more time. *I* need a drink myself.

"Valium?!" I almost yell. "Are you sure?"

"It helps me down. Otherwise it's horrible. They didn't leave me alone. Someone was with me twenty-four hours a day."

Alone. It's my fault. I left him alone in that far-flung tangle, in the sticks. And now he's still alone in D.C., all messed up. But, stupid me, he's been alone for years. He went off to college by himself; came home in the summers, handled his own life, did his own applications for the Peace Corps. By himself. As it should be. Alone.

"But don't worry, Mom. We're working out a plan. I've got a counselor here and we're figuring it all out. I've gotta get back to my village fast—as soon as we get this thing settled. I don't crave alcohol, really. It's just a problem when I drink; I react badly. There's some sorta abnormality there. I think they overreacted when they flew me out but it's just Peace Corps protocol. The thing they do."

"Yeah," I say as offhandedly as I can. Are there any cheap flights to D.C. from Seattle? After all, I haven't seen him in nine months. Not that I could change a thing. But just to hug him. To say it will be okay. That's what I need. And isn't this about *me*, this call to *my* kitchen?

"I've gotta go, Mom," he slurs. "I have homework. The counselor wants to see my journal writing. I'm typing it out for him. And I'll email you a copy. Right away. I'll call you tomorrow. I love you."

When I left for the market earlier today, my son was living in South America working for the Peace Corps. By the time I returned home to put the groceries away, he'd become an alcoholic headed for rehab. So what happened between the produce aisle and my driveway? Toren's father, Don, is at work. He would want to know about this situation. I could call him at the hospital. I could email him since he picks up messages in the OR between cases. The subject title should be—"Sit Down." There's no granite counter in the operating room.

So, do I start at the end or the beginning when I tell him? It's hard to know just where we are.

3

CRYING COUCH

As far as we could tell, Toren had completed the requisite Peace Corps training in the first months of 2003, embraced his assignment, and was adapting to life in South America. He told us funny stories on the phone and related that he was very involved with his village family, just 'living' and following people around at whatever tasks they were doing. He felt extremely busy each day. We asked him what he did, and he said that, for example, yesterday he'd gone with a twenty-year-old guy into a cornfield. They picked corn, husked it, cut off the kernels, mashed the kernels, then made some smushy, sweet corn-cakes, cooked them, and ate them. He also caught some chickens, killed them, plucked them, and after our conversation, was going to eat one of them with the family.

"I'm like another kid in the family," he said. "They don't think I can do anything. The first time I whistled, they were astounded. 'Look! He already knows how to whistle.' The children think that I'm not only stupid, but blind because I wear glasses. The little niña comes up to me and holds three fingers in front of my face really close, and says, 'How many?' And when I answer with a bad accent or slowly, she yells, 'See, I told you he can't see!'" Toren wanted to tell the family that he does actually know some things, but he couldn't speak clearly in the indigenous language.

"It's hopeless," he sighed. He survived by just playing along. He said if he picked up an orange, they'd rip it out of his hand and explain how to peel an orange to him. They believed he had a low IQ because they had never seen anyone his age who couldn't talk.

Toren originally thought that he would move to his own place sooner, but now he understood that in order to survive, there were a lot of skills he needed to acquire, including speech. So living with a helpful family had been ideal at the beginning.

Though frustrated by his language skills, Toren was very positive about his situation and happy to immerse himself in his new life there. He laughed when we talked about visiting him sometime in 2004, but felt that 99 percent of the people he knew in the U.S. wouldn't be stimulated by his lifestyle or living circumstances. Toren found himself extremely busy and supported by the people around him. With so much to learn, he was satisfied to concentrate on day-to-day life. He had recently moved into his own house and was cultivating a garden. That was all we knew about his life.

When he left for the Peace Corps in January of 2003, Toren took two books along with him: *The Complete Works of William Shakespeare* and a book of Spanish verbs. He lamented over leaving his drum set behind, but purchased a guitar as soon as possible after arriving in South America. To pay for three months of intensive Spanish Language training in southern Mexico prior to his induction into the Peace Corps, he'd used his own money from his summer employment.

Immediately after college graduation and prior to leaving for Peace Corps, Toren had chosen to live on his own in Seattle close to his summertime landscaping job. He shared living expenses with friends. (Our family policy was that once you finished college, you supported yourself, which included paying for your own health and auto insurance, your food, and your housing.) In September, he moved to Las Vegas to live with his two brothers for a few weeks prior to attending a language school in Mexico. Our extended family, with all the grandparents, aunts, uncles and cousins, planned to spend Christmas in Mazatlán, so Toren met us there directly after his studies and travel in Mexico. There he spent the week reading stories to his young cousins, talking with grandparents and aunts, and partying at night with his brothers.

When the rest of the family departed for home after Christmas, Toren returned to Las Vegas and San Diego to pick up his personal belongings, then flew to Seattle to stay with Don and me the final week before his Peace Corps departure. There were last minute arrangements to finalize and supplies to purchase. Toren was allowed a limited amount of luggage and faced decisions about equipment that needed to last two years and three months, his assigned term of service.

We spent a great week together even though he came home looking rather bedraggled. I remember being perturbed with his lack of physical and mental preparation, but I thought it was because he was having difficulty coping with the length of his impending absence, that he needed to say farewell to all his friends and brothers in grand style. I tried to overlook his spaciness, figuring he was young and insecure. Don and I drove him to the airport and felt a real ache as he strode onto the plane to begin his training.

Upon his January arrival in South America we didn't communicate often. The mail service was sporadic. Over fifteen letters mailed from the U.S. had never reached Toren, and his email connection was an hour's walk from his village. Our best means of communication was by phone so Toren usually had us call him about once every six weeks.

I noticed in July and August that Toren's already infrequent emails had become even more erratic. He lacked enthusiasm when we spoke with him on the phone. He seemed scattered. I asked his brothers if they heard from Toren often, if they thought he was okay. No one suspected problems. But I sensed that Toren was avoiding returning my emails and I worried that something was brooding under the surface.

In August, I wrote him a rather terse letter where I requested he respond to us, that he answer our emails, and I pointed out that he had yet to mail us even one letter! I felt guilty for doing this because Peace Corps had warned parents about expecting too much in the first year while the volunteer is in a big adjustment phase.

When Don and I called South America in late August to talk with Toren about scheduling a visit in May 2004, Toren was vague about when we should come and seemed less than welcoming. This was not the cheerful Toren I remembered. In retrospect, I realize that by that time, he was coming to terms with his alcoholism, deciding what to do about it.

So that was the part we knew.

The part of Toren's life we didn't know was what he had now confessed to me on the kitchen phone, the long-time alcohol abuse. And even more blatant, a portion we knew very little about was what he subsequently emailed to us from his journal, *My Drink*. This was the other side of Toren, the aspect that sent me into a frenzied state of misery. I had no idea he would divulge such unbearable news.

My first reaction to Toren's announcement was shock. I began sifting through memories of the recent past, wondering what clues I had missed. Then, my angst mounted. The days following Toren's initial phone call caused intense agitation and despair. I moped and tearfully told myself this wasn't about me, it was about Toren. But in my heart and soul, I knew how connected we were and that whatever affected Toren also became a part of me and a part of our family. At the same time, I knew Toren's strength and will, and I knew his optimism. He definitely had a challenge before him, a life-long one, and if he could formulate a consistent plan, I was positive he would triumph.

Had I known more about alcoholism, I may not have been so optimistic at this point. I'd had a few friends go through rehab and I remembered that their recovery involved permanent changes of behavior. I hoped Toren could do that.

Don and I took this stumble very hard and we took it together. Actually, it was more than a stumble, it was a downslide into a chasm, causing us to look at our lifestyle and how much our social interactions needlessly revolved around alcohol. Suddenly it seemed that everything we did involved meeting for a beer or having a glass of wine. We spent time discussing how this alcohol problem interlocked in the puzzle of our family. I tried to think of it as Toren's gift to us, the chance to reflect on all of this and to talk with our other boys about substance abuse.

We checked out both the Alcoholics Anonymous (AA) and the Al-Anon websites in our search for information. AA is an organization well known throughout the world. Its members' primary purpose is to stay sober and help other alcoholics to achieve sobriety. I found there also exists a group called Narcotics Anonymous (NA) which employs AA principles, but was founded for drug users. NA maintains that alcohol is a recognized addictive substance, no different from heroin, cocaine or other drugs or combinations of drugs. And to help the families of alcoholics, Al-Anon and Alateen were also founded. I glanced at the Twelve Steps and figured I ought to learn more about these concepts if Toren would be studying them, also. The Steps seemed foreign to me, yet reasonable. I found it hard to imagine attending an Al-Anon meeting.

Toren's life suddenly seemed out of our control. And out of Toren's control. Decisions were being made about his future while I was home grinding coffee beans and vacuuming car mats. There was nothing I could do about it. It was frustrating having no means to communicate with Toren. We didn't even know his phone number. We were dependent upon his calls from Washington, D.C., calls telling us of the drastic decisions being made about his life, determinations made for him by total strangers. I hoped that this team of competent professionals could help him to deal with his dilemma. Better than I.

It was all the more painful for us, being unable to talk with anyone else about this sudden news. Toren had asked us not to divulge this incident to anyone, and we were abiding by that. He wanted people to think he was still in South America. He said there was still the hope he could go back and no one would know any different. So we held our peace. Don and I possessed a large support system in our town, and we were unable to utilize it. We truly leaned on one another at this point.

Sleepless nights haunted me. I wondered how Toren was doing, where he was in Washington, D.C., what he was deciding. I wondered how I could have let this happen. My pacing often lead me to the boys' shared upstairs bedroom where I would bury myself on their couch, wrapped in an afghan, weeping at what had become of our Perfect Family.

I made a List of Worries:

1. That I will lose a child.

2. That I can't help my child.
3. That my child has gone astray.
4. That my child is hopeless.
5. That my child is paralyzed.
6. That I can't make him better.
7. That my child is making bad choices.
8. That my child is in pain.
9. That my child feels alone.
10. That I don't know where he is.
11. That I can't concentrate.
12. That I feel despair.
13. That I threw everything into raising my child, but it didn't help.
14. That my child doesn't see his own potential.
15. That I am judging my success by my child's deeds.
16. That I thought he'd be 'launched' by now.
17. That my child is closing doors on himself.
18. That I failed to recognize my child's needs.
19. That I didn't provide necessary structure for:
    ✓ fiscal judgment
    ✓ self esteem
    ✓ ability to execute a plan
    ✓ avoidance of substance abuse
20. That I don't know what to do next.

I read my list to Don the next morning. He put his arm around me and advised, "Chris, you can't be the poor devastated mother-victim. Pull yourself out of this. No one is going to feel sorry for you. No one wants to hear about it."

"But I *am* a failure. I totally screwed up," I sobbed to him. The Breathalyzer, the nights waiting up for them in high school, the family projects, the discussions. It was as if our efforts to raise a solid family had never happened. It was like the boys ran out and immediately did everything we advised them not to do. Surely if one son was an alcoholic, maybe they all were. I probably hadn't found out about the rest of them yet. "I feel like a CEO who spends her whole life building up a corporation to find out no one she's trained is capable." Where is my crying couch?

Repeat: "You can't be the poor devastated mother, Chris." My husband looked as miserable as I.

"Just imagine how you would feel," I said, "if, after all these years of practicing medicine, suddenly one-third of all your healthy patients either died or had life-threatening complications while in the OR, even though you were practicing the best medicine possible and doing everything in your power to have a successful outcome. Wouldn't you feel personally responsible? It's been your career to manage them well, to help them! Moreover, what if the remaining two-thirds were also in jeopardy? Suddenly you may have all your patients at risk of death or life-long problems. How do you feel now? So let me mourn," I told my husband. "Let me have my bad times here in the privacy of my home." He hugged me and smiled, his own eyes tearing.

And he let me be. For the next two weeks I hovered close to home, refusing to answer the phone, reading and writing, practicing the viola, thinking and thinking and wondering what the hell had happened. My lack of composure made me avoid most of my friends. I was afraid they would see how upset I was. People always say that a parent isn't to blame for what a child does, but when this parent has purposely elected to stay home in order to raise and nurture a child, a poor outcome is relatively incriminating. To me the cause of the problem was not clear at all, except that it had to be something that took place in our home. The crying couch had a lot of business for a few days. I just couldn't help it.

It was selfish to fixate on this problem. On the overall scale of global misery, the dilemma of my alcoholic son was relatively low. But to me, it was catastrophic. Owning up to having raised an alcoholic child would be devastating to every mother, regardless of whether she was stay-at-home or career-oriented. Any parent, mother or father, would feel the stigma and pain of suddenly realizing an addict had been reared in the household. Now I needed to determine what I could do to bolster the esteem of our parenting, to make sure that my actions were looking forward, not backward. I knew this, but for the moment, I was overwhelmed by the grief of what the last nine years signified.

During my wake of our family's innocence, Toren called twice more. The very next day, he answered more of our questions about his final days in South America. The majority of his drinking, he said, had been with fellow volunteers when they would meet on occasional weekends. The drinking occurred at a social level outside the jurisdiction of Peace Corps work. Toren described to us how medical supervisors from the Peace Corps helped him detox, then how a few days later they drove him in a private car (his first real auto ride in nine months) on dirt roads to his village where he packed his things and locked his house.

"Did you get all your stuff?" I asked him.

"No. There's still some there. It was so rushed. I felt sick, it was confusing., it was hell. I couldn't say good-bye to anyone in my village because I arrived so suddenly, packed, then…I just left in that car."

"Did anyone in your village know about this?"

"No. I didn't really drink in my village, except for a few times. I hadn't had any problems there because I didn't drink there much. I told my South American mother that I had a family emergency. I gave her my keys. I had to leave all my ideas for projects, my new family, my friends. I had to leave my life there."

"Will anyone go back for your belongings?"

"I haven't given up on that yet. *I* want to go back. I know I can."

"But Toren, it sounds like they want you to go into treatment. Isn't that what you've told us?"

"The Peace Corps tricked me into leaving. I wouldn't have gone to the nurse if I'd thought they would make me leave South America. So they have to let me return. It's just that I react badly to alcohol. They need to tell me how to fix the problem so I can go back. I know I have a problem, but I can handle it. I *have* to get back to South America. I didn't get to say good-bye."

4

My Drink

by Toren Volkmann

21 May 2003

Age 23

A long night of drinking used to make me tired...now it makes me stay up and shake. I'm an alcoholic. I guess drinking like an alcoholic for about eight or nine years was part of the problem. Luckily, it was fun as hell.

Now what? Cocaine? How can I find a new identity when I used to drink mine by the fluid ounce and then turn around and juggle reality?

I thought the problem with being an alcoholic was you just drank a lot. I did that just fine and things were great. No one ever said, "Dude, you're gonna start losing your money, your memory and, above all, your longevity and tolerance..." as if just being shit-faced and happy every night weren't enough, "...and when you stop a mean bender you're going to be a fevering, shaky, paranoid halfwit for a day or two who can't think, sleep, even relax or eat until withdrawals are over...." That page of my D.A.R.E book must have been ripped out, right after the one part I do remember that said all the bad kids always had fun and got all the chicks.

I used to be able to handle the worst of hangovers, wear it like a soldier wore a uniform, or drink it off. I could deal with hellacious sleeplessness from drinking for a day or through the night, maybe ending up in some random bed and still charging through class, ball practice or family happenings like the dark angel that I was...even the torrential blackouts that would be reported or random acts of split personality. My friends and I always gave ourselves alternate drinking names (My name was Poren), as a joke, saying, "So and so did that, not *me.*" It was nothing to be ashamed of in 'the glory days.' Things are changing and what I once thirsted for and sucked on with the finest appreciation, shared with the warmest of friends in the best and most fucked-up times, is beginning to scare me.

It's not the urge to drink that I don't have power over—this hasn't been the case (24 pack where are you?). Rather, what was once all benefit and reward—raging parties, boring conversation turned into passionate arguments, blaring music and endless cigarettes, slurring exchanges of understanding (or even unfaithful or unwarranted kisses)—now seems to be packaged with much more unpredictability; I now have increased difficulty controlling my level of intoxication.

More importantly, there is an equal reaction corresponding to the amount of alcohol consumed in regard to the eventual detox. This is the big problem. During detox, inside the unsettled body, a nervous and sometimes nauseous sense begins...an anxiety and almost a fear, like being too alone. You see yourself and everything differently. Like a sudden collapse of the stock market of your brain and every single nerve ending in your body wants to turn inside-out and puke out some unidentifiable pain or itch. You sweat, and you sweat increasingly when you let unreasonable thoughts trick you into feeling like whatever you are thinking must be true, like for example, (hhhhmm...) maybe another drink will solve the problem.

I went to college each year and would return home for summer break to live with my folks and work by day as a groundskeeper. But really, I lived for the weekends, and everything worked out perfectly that way. I would go up to Seattle and rock all weekend, hardly eating and just shooting the shit (loving it always), cracking beers from the early morning, and turning over what was remaining from the previous night. The weekends were endless parties, fiascos, adventures. And always intoxicating.

That last summer at home, I grew to hate Monday mornings at work, or sometimes Tuesday, too. It wasn't due to a headache or hating work. I liked being outside and listening to all the jack-offs on talk radio with their big opinions and constant advertising. But more and more, I would be tired. Sunday nights or Monday nights I would find myself in bed at 9 or 10 p.m., knowing that I may not get to sleep until 4, 5 or 6 a.m. My legs would cramp sometimes, or ache depending on how bad it was, or how much I had drunk. I'd have sweaty, sudden convulsions just as my body began to relax or fall asleep. I would be scared to fall asleep and lay awake frightened, having no clue what to do, in total dread until it would finally subside enough to let me sleep. HELL. I tried to think it was normal, but I knew something was up. Little did I know it was the start of something that I would slowly come to realize was part of my reality. It was my penance after coming off another celebratory binge. This reaction slowly progressed over the last two years of college.

The first time I ever noticed that I had the shakes and didn't attribute it to lack of food was in 2000, my sophomore year of college...not even twenty-one years old. I was trying to fix a tangled cassette. Unfortunately, my hand was vibrating, so I gave myself some wine and was able to enjoy the tape along with the rest of the wine, after both problems were 'fixed.' Buzzed and horrified, I called my brother and recounted to him what had happened as if I'd just had my first wet dream or some other eventual rite of passage to manhood. Unsurprised, if I remember, I think he more or less welcomed me to the club or alluded to the idea of 'Where have you been?' That made me feel better as did the rest of the boxed wine, but the progression has proved to be a nightmare.

I made it through college just fine and, from what I remember, it was the time of my life. I have a lot of really screwed-up pictures, a black book, and valuable friendships to prove it. I became very disheartened with my difficult routine by the end, though. My senior year was awfully tough. Getting blitzed every weekend was amazing and coming back to the dorms on campus was always an interesting disaster.

I used to tell people, the few who understood, how my ridiculous schedule went:

SCHIZOPHRENIC MONDAY:
Inferior to myself, no schoolwork, too preoccupied and on edge...easily startled by common things, vulnerable, and self esteem at negative ten.

WORRY TUESDAY:
Still fevering, thinking of how I am gonna magically execute all that reading, classes, papers, exams—brilliantly done in the end, I must add.
WHATEVER WEDNESDAY:
How much I really drank last weekend=how I function this day.
PRODUCTIVE THURSDAY:
Back on track and kicking ass, do it all, I AM school.
FUCKING FRIDAY:
Sense of humor fully restored, all energy and in gear...just in time to start the cycle all over again...pattern here?????????????

This gave me about two or three days of productivity. So on Fridays I would delve into bliss, oblivion, carelessness, and a state of being that defied concern; one that was mostly impossible for the average student or peer. Satisfactorily saturated, self-sufficient and in need of nothing more than my friends and my cheap booze (211, 40s, ice beers, and maybe some high class malt liquor); I was set. I would drink the empties of all the leftover beers (wounded soldiers) people left (the ones who probably went home early) and I'd wonder, 'What was their problem?' Well, whatever those 'normal' people did, they didn't seem to catch 'my' disease. It must be something towards the bottom of the bottle that did it. Anyway, I had the best of times. Simplicity—lots of rocking music, drinking games, and companionship. Done deal. No bars or girl chasing, just laughs, craziness and comfort. Where was the problem? [See SCHIZOPHRENIC MONDAY]

At this point in my life, I'm not sure if this is a disease or not [it is]. I chose it and loved it. If I choose to drink like I did before, the symptoms that ensue are surely my fault. I am simply struggling with the aftermath of the next good time that I want to have. Why does detox have to exist and be sooooo painful, making one struggle to talk, and even lose his sense of humor? These are the functions alcohol usually eases for people, now the results are the opposite. It has me totally puzzled and unsure how to explain it, mainly to the ones I care about, and also the ones who may be alcoholics, too.

After I graduated from college the summer of 2002, I moved

up to Seattle to live with some old friends from high school. To save words, I again put into action what I did best. I drank—almost every day. No more school, a bad job market, and man, it was perfect. Even better, there were World Cup Soccer matches on TV every night to keep me wasted until five in the morning. GOOAAALLLL!!!!!

Eventually I started landscaping and I still went hard every night, partying. It didn't seem to matter. I woke up with vigor and readiness. I packed my lunch, and then would get stuck in traffic with my music and a cigarette knowing that I could work, get money, and go home to good friends and drinks. And those were my summer weekdays. The weekends were ten times better with girls and parties, concerts or occasional visits to Olympia. There wasn't a care in the world, and I never had to come down.

Sometimes I would start to come down—maybe I didn't drink much the night before or had an appointment or family dinner—I snuck by without drinking or even nursing a few down and I'd start slipping into a DT [a delirium tremen; a severe type of withdrawal]. In these moments, with a wet and hot/cold forehead, I'd find it difficult to focus on the task at hand, like remembering that I was supposed to bring something to the car or not knowing what I had just talked about with someone for ten minutes. My inability to recall details was very annoying and, the further into withdrawal I would get, the more frustrations turned into fears, anxieties, loss of confidence and purpose, and even worse, a disappearing sense of humor. These are the kinds of shit that compose your personality and when they suddenly start to change or disappear it is freaky and no fun. It seems totally beyond control—purely physical.

The summer ended with the whole crew of friends seeming to have graduated, changed locations, or split up to travel or whatever. I had signed myself up to go with the U.S. Government for two years, hopefully to South America. It was not to fight in the armed forces but to serve as a volunteer. This gave me several months to kill, and I would almost literally do this.

I spent the better part of September and October of 2002 in Las Vegas, and at times on road trips to the coast—mainly to touch base with all my study buddies, right? My biggest plan was

to spend time with my two brothers who worked in
visit friends in San Diego. I have tried to recount an
the nights and different trips to San Diego and it is
impossible. Invariably we had a blast and I was losing great chunks
of each night, either corresponding to a.) how much fun we had
or b.) how much of a jackass I (Poren) 'may' have been.

I drank every night in Vegas, too. It was great. We raged
through the casinos, walked down the crowded strip with our
sleazy malt liquors and cheap half-racks, almost rubbing in the fact
that we could do such a thing in front of such 'classy' gambling
folks. On our better nights, we would then find ourselves at the
trashy Gold Spike Casino, giggling and doing penny slots super
early in the morning. Luckily, we knew gambling was another issue
we didn't need. Besides, every time you give the Seven-Eleven
cashier 99 cents, you know you get a tall can of 24-ounce Steel
Reserve or malt liquor that'll get you just that much more
intoxicated. Where's the gamble in that?

Eventually, I went down to Oaxaca, Mexico to study Spanish
in preparation for my upcoming service in South America. Upon
arrival, I was met with the harshest of withdrawals, which magnified
everything that I have previously described. I spent two solid nights
in hotels, only going out to find water and a banana, hoping not
to be noticed or to have to talk while aiming to remember where
my room was with all my stuff. After those two days I proceeded
to 'recover'—a valued word for this topic—and basically stayed
away from alcohol all but two or three times in six weeks. The
clarity was quick in coming, comforting and surprisingly easy. But
still, I knew my reality was scary.

From this point on, I think something hit me and began telling
me 'I can never, at least physically, go back to the way it was.' I
knew that, not just monetarily, but physically, I would pay for
every drink or intoxicatingly good time I would have. Meeting
my family for Christmas in Mexico after eight weeks of language
class (and some travel with a few slip-ups, we'll say) was perfect—
a chance to say good-bye before leaving for two years. I showed
up sober and beyond any chance of withdrawal. My bro's pulled
in from Vegas with carry-on bags under their eyes and the scent
of a great night on their breath. I was amazed and jealous at the

same time. But they didn't seem in too bad of shape. How? I couldn't have done that.

The first two days or so with the family were great. I remember sitting with one of my brothers at a table during sunset watching my uncle and cousins surf fishing in the shallow waves. We were talking, smiling, sharing a beer, and savoring a perfect moment. How things should be.

How could the situation change?

"Paging Doctor Toren Volkmann, please report to your own personal disaster called Alcoholism—the tremors, sweats, and antisocial symptoms will be right with you."

Sure enough, after a few hard drinks (tequila that tasted like it had been made in a bathtub), the process began to start—paranoid, confused, intoxicated *me* showed up, tetering on the edge of withdrawal. This side of detox is the one that turns a regular conversation into a task, even if it is with the closest of friends, it doesn't matter. Although they might not notice, inside me is another whole world of pain. The anxiety and difficulty that exists depends on the level of alcohol—alcohol either previously consumed or alcohol in deficit.

After Mexico, I had one last stint in San Diego before my final good-bye with my brothers in Las Vegas. I don't remember shit for the most part and even skipped out on seeing some of my most important friends because I was too gone to really care or make an effort to contact some of them. As it turned out, thanks to a stolen disposable camera and Satan himself, some pictures revealed that I did actually see a few of them. Silly ol' me.

That last morning in San Diego I found myself driving to Vegas in a borrowed car with a gal I didn't know too well. We stopped once, and talked about the same number of times. Although sleepless, I knew that my good old withdrawals wouldn't let me relax so I was confident I would not fall asleep at the wheel. I even let the same CD repeat over and over because I felt too sick and stupid to suggest that we put in another.

The more days in a row I would drink, the more easily these symptoms would surface, and the more intensely they hindered my normal relaxed style of thinking and way of interacting with others. It really started to steal my enthusiasm, my aura, and my soul. I probably could have looked into a mirror and seen the back wall at times, things seemed so bad. This was not the life I'd ordered.

During my final Las Vegas days, I kept a steady supply in me and generally had a good time. Previous months studying in Mexico had made me realize that my drinking situation was worse than I thought. Drinking now emerged as both my solution and my problem. In opportune moments I think I tried to hint to both my brothers that I was bothered by some of the shit that 'it' was doing to me—they're my fucking brothers! They know what 'it' is and what I'm talking about. But maybe they didn't...What I was trying to tell them surely didn't really come out clearly. In fact, nothing came out conclusively because I didn't want to say it. If the first step to beating the problem is admitting it or accepting it, I guess I just didn't want to beat anything quite yet. Why the hell did it have to be so bad all of the sudden?

Leaving Las Vegas was maybe the low point to this day, [interjection: things did get lower since writing this] in my new 'dialogue' with alcohol. On the floor that last morning, I woke up all too early—which often happens when the body starts losing its normal equilibrium of alcohol—lying next to a girl I really cared for. We may have actually had sex the previous night (if I could only piece together a few simple clues with some certainty.) The fact is that I totally slept with her, we knew I was leaving for two years, and she wanted to talk about it. Experiencing withdrawals, uncomfortable and unable to sleep, I tried to act asleep to avoid the whole situation which should have been a memorable good-bye. I didn't know what the hell to say and I felt like crap. It only made me feel worse hiding my problem from her and sweating out the hours that should have been shared between friends.

With few hours left in Vegas, my problem was worsening without drinks, and I had to tear down whatever I wanted from our tastelessly covered walls and pack for my departure and upcoming disappearance. Good-byes are always difficult but what ensued was terrible. I look back on it with sadness and regret. I tried but couldn't even smile or appreciate our final moments, or express the joy, the love I had for my brothers and my friends. I was too lost in fevers, trembles, and general ineptness, and I felt like they all could see right through it. I was out of my mind. I was scared to leave, and scared of what was happening inside me. It was killing me and was all wrong for no reason; life is supposed to be great.

Eventually, I boarded a plane home to Seattle, my body in pain, shaking, and my legs aching. Behind me, all the way, a baby shrieked as if to express my exact state of being while magnifying it at the same time. I could barely tolerate to sit, stand, think—live. My mom picked me up at the airport and I played it off legit. It was a tough ride home, trying to read letters about my Peace Corps assignment in South America, making normal conversation that made no sense to me, only wanting to disappear.

I had two days to 'relax' and a night of non-sleep, like so many previous nights during those wild Seattle summers, before the symptoms slowly subsided. I didn't even try to start packing for South America, knowing any brainless attempt would just provoke sweaty confusion and stress. I was worthless. I could barely explain pictures of my trip to Mexico to my parents because I was still so affected by the recovery from that latest binge I had put myself through. Why was it so hard? Was this really necessary?

In my hometown in early January 2003, with a bit more time before leaving, I wiggled my way out of seeing most of my old high school friends and drinking buddies. I wanted to be sane in my final days before departing for the Peace Corps in order to prepare myself. Yes, by then I had learned what happens when I drink, but it wasn't over yet. Being sober, I was able to find myself and deal with my rational fears of leaving the country for two years with logic and confidence in myself. But departing to another continent by no means left my problem behind.

The question is: What do I do now? How can I make this work? What I can't help but wonder is whether all those famous [dead] rock stars, winos on the streets, or some of my best friends have experienced these types of things or are experiencing them now? Maybe they just never said so or aren't admitting it. Maybe what I experience is much different from others. But I can't imagine anyone bearing the internal hell that I feel as a result of hard drinking and continuing on without letting others know. How did I not ever hear about this side of alcohol and withdrawal? For me, the silence is over and it is time to start looking for answers. I am also looking for the right cliché to end this—Bottoms up!!

Originally written: 5-21-03   South America
Updated: 9-23-03   Washington DC

5

BREWING A PLAN

SHE KNEW WHAT IT WAS LIKE TO FALL BACK INTO THE INNER DARKNESS OF THE
SELF. TO IMPLODE NIGHTS AND COME TO EVERY MORNING LIKE RECONSTITUTED
MISERY. COME CRAWLING BACK IN THE DAY CELL OF THE PUNY WITHERING
BODY. SHE KNEW ALL ABOUT THE BLACK HOLES OF THE SELF.

THOM JONES, *COLD SNAP* [4]

23 SEPTEMBER 2003. FOR THE FIRST TIME I OPEN TOREN'S *My Drink*
email, forewarned about the content. As I read, the walls of our
house rise off the foundation and a vapid emptiness surrounds the
raising of my children. I sit at my computer, staring at tough words
describing our son's alienation from all we had attempted to offer.
Even greater is my grief at his silent suffering, his grappling with
learning how to detox himself, on his own. I recall the times he
splayed uselessly on our couch, peering through his own sweat at
nature videos. Over and over. And I now realize my ignorance. I feel
foolish and inept. I undergo such inner remorse that I cannot move
away from the tangle of his words. So I read them again.

A sudden visceral reaction causes me to detest alcohol. I wish to
remove it all from our house. At the same time, I want to pour myself
the largest glass of Scotch in the world and gulp it down as fast as I
can. Suddenly, I hate alcohol. I despise what it has done to our family.
And I worry about Toren's brothers, if they may be in the same gurgling
boat.

By the time my husband Don returns home, Toren calls again
from Washington, D.C. He is trying to make a decision about his

treatment and wants us to talk to Carl, a counselor assigned to him by the Peace Corps. Carl connects us for a telephone conference with Toren. We're talking together as if we were executives making a touchy policy decision. My husband and I speak on separate phones in our home, our boys' pictures splashed on desktops and shelves, grinning at us while we decide where our youngest should be sent, like determining the best concentration camp or jail cell. Carl tells us the team has been assessing Toren's level of disease and he informs us that Toren has been classified as an alcoholic.

"Of course, you knew he was an alcoholic," Carl states.

Did we? I want to say, No, no, we didn't. We're shocked. But Carl has already moved on. Doesn't Carl know we haven't lived under the same roof with our son for five years? How could we 'know?' Maybe we did. I'm trying to defend myself and be agreeable all at once. There isn't time to decide whether I knew or not. I must have known. He's my son, isn't he?

And then Carl emphasizes, "If ever Toren is to return to the Peace Corps as a recovering alcoholic, he must first stay sober for three years." In a matter of seconds, before my very eyes, Toren has evolved from slick college grad volunteer to a failing alcoholic, and now suddenly Carl is calling Toren a *recovering* alcoholic. It's like a miracle. Toren's *already* recovering before I even perceived he *was* an alcoholic!

Three years. It sounds like an eternity to not drink alcohol. Don and I drink it several times a week. I picture Toren going three years without it and I can't imagine. This Carl must have high hopes. And before I can catch my breath, he goes on to say that Toren is eligible for inpatient therapy (with a success rate of 80 percent after one year) or he could do outpatient (with a 20 percent success rate after one year). Carl maintains that Toren is ahead of the game because he already acknowledges that he's an alcoholic. He is motivated, he turned himself in. Most of Carl's clients, he says, have to be hauled into rehab kicking and screaming. I don't hear any sounds from Toren. Maybe he's sitting there tied up. It's just Don, me and Carl talking about Toren as though he were a slab of jerky. We go on to discuss the rehab facility recommended by Carl, which Carl says is not a lock-up facility, how it's spiritually based and 12-Step oriented, and that there's a family education program. Such Amenities. I'm thinking all this time, what am I going to tell my mother? And did Toren have a window or an aisle seat on his plane flight out of South America? I want to be a bad girl. If I'm naughty, Carl will go away and I won't have to hear all this wrenching news. Carl won't want to work with me. He and Toren can figure it out without me. It's hard to concentrate on all this information which seems to be overtaking the world I'd envisioned.

Carl tells us that Toren thinks he's at a nine out of ten level of awareness in understanding his alcohol problem. Whereas Carl maintains Toren is actually at a level four out of ten. Toren listens to all this as we yak about him and I wonder if he wants to add anything. Maybe he's still on Valium. I strain to hear his breathing. He must be amazed at how, just two days ago, he resided in South America digging roots, and now he's deported to the nation's capitol talking on the phone to his parents and an addiction expert. Carl has been doing this sort of thing for fifteen years and tells us he "puts away" about twenty-five people a year. He has about one person every three years like Toren who turns himself in, the rest have to be wrestled in.

Carl is very professional and I can tell he's trying to let us down easy when he breaks the news that, most likely, Toren will be discharged from the Peace Corps. But here Toren cuts in, "Wait a minute. I'll do the rehab, but let's not close the doors on returning to South America!" He sounds agitated, determined.

But Carl retorts that they've already tried sending people back to Peace Corps in the past. It has never worked because the job is too isolated and there's not enough support for recovery. Recovery— there's that word again—such an optimistic term. I wonder how Carl can throw it out there so easily, before our son has even started. I'm barely used to the fact that Toren's an alcoholic. How can I even begin thinking of his recovery? But maybe Toren's recovery is already starting, the fact that he sought help. I try to get hopeful with the phone glued to my ear. I want to cooperate with Carl, really. He's being so helpful.

"Liquor in South America's too cheap and too available. Toren would plummet," Carl warns. He says 100 percent not to count on Toren going back before three years of sobriety.

Toren asserts that he still wants to return to his project. He maintains that just because the Peace Corps has tried returning people unsuccessfully in prior years doesn't mean it won't work with him. He's positive that he will succeed. It's quiet a few seconds before Toren says, "Okay, I'll go into inpatient therapy. But I want to have a discussion *afterwards* about returning to South America."

Carl responds to us and to Toren saying, "I don't want Toren going into rehab focusing on returning to South America. Instead, Toren needs to focus on alcohol addiction and his disease and learning what to do about it. He needs to meditate, to gain spirituality." Carl won't budge.

From my end of the phone connection I can tell that Toren is fuming about abandoning South America, but resigned for the present. "I don't have a choice at this point," Toren concedes. "I'm going." He chuckles and I wonder what could possibly be amusing.

Toren agrees to sign a contract saying that if he decides to quit the program, he will contact Carl first. Carl will make the final recommendation on Toren's status after the twenty-eight day program, and reminds us again that if Toren can stay sober for three years, he could have a chance to re-enter the Peace Corps one day. He wants Toren to begin the rehab program on Thursday, September 25th. Tomorrow. Carl feels we shouldn't waste any time. Toren will be driven there. We won't hear from him for over one week. If Toren has problems, he'll call Carl. The first week is very hard, apparently.

What could be hard about one week in comparison to the last nine months of hell?

Don and I hang up and rush to one another. We're dry-eyed. It's worse than we'd thought. We had no idea. How could we have missed it? We both realize there's nothing we can do about this. It's already happened.

"I'm not going to drink while Toren's in rehab," I tell Don. "I want to support him."

31

"Okay. I'll do it, too," Don says. And suddenly we both recognize that there'll be no wine with dinner this evening. No gin and tonic on the end of the dock at sunset. Even though it's Wednesday and we don't drink during the week, maybe tonight we would have, since it was such a stressful day. But we've made the decision. And that's final. If we can't do this for twenty-eight days, how do we expect our son to do it the rest of his life?

I have symphony rehearsal anyway. And wouldn't you know, after rehearsal, a friend invites me out for a beer. She and I have performed in the viola section for twenty years. We're string player nerds, but usually we go out once every six weeks. I tell her yes, and when we sit at the bar and I order a soft drink she asks me, "Chris, are you okay?"

And now I understand how the next twenty-eight days will go. I want to say, "Yes, I'm fine. I'm not drinking because I'm supporting my son in rehab."

But I remember that Toren has asked us to keep this news in the family; he wants only his brothers and us to know about it. "Because," he conjectures, "maybe when I finish rehab, I'll go back to South America and no one will know I left."

I blunder through my fizzy non-mood-altering drink. And my fellow musician senses my malaise. She knows me too well. I steer all conversation away from our family, hoping she won't ask how Toren's doing. We talk about her kids, her classroom where she teaches, the music for the upcoming concert. Soon it's time to leave. I wonder how I will ever survive twenty-eight days of deceit with my friends. I will be forced to lie.

The next month cannot pass too quickly for me. On Saturday it's 80 degrees, most unusual for late September in the Pacific Northwest. Our bay waters are a sublime blue and Don is out in the early morning setting crab traps for our dinner. We will eat alone on our beach before a fire and talk about Toren, our family, and our life in this intimate universe of missteps and giant leaps.

I remember how, as a child, I often played 'Mother, may I?' in the backyard with my sisters and neighbors. There were many kinds of maneuvers we invented to get to the finish line: banana steps, scissor steps, baby steps, giant steps. And sometimes we tried to cheat, to get away with something if we thought we could. If we made it across the line before anyone else, we won. Somehow, we got there. It was a game of preparation, of contortion. Of surviving the best way we could.

Don and I call Toren's brothers. Toren has asked us to let them know. Even though he wants to call them himself, he has limited phone time. "Your brother isn't in South America," we begin. And we spit it out about Toren's alcoholism.

"Are you sure there isn't a mistake?" one brother asks from Alabama where he's in school for his Masters Program. Twenty-six years old, he visited Toren in his South American village just two months prior. Certainly he would have sensed this overwhelming problem. We tell him it was Toren's own idea to confess. He listens to us and doesn't say much, realizing that what's happening will not be changed by a brother's opinion. After the next call to the oldest, our twenty-seven year old son who lives in Nevada, we are finished informing.

Each of us must learn the news and sort through the facts of Toren's disease for ourselves. Toren has decided to go into an inpatient rehab program, and none of us have lived in his skin. We cannot tell him whether it is right or wrong. Both brothers will soon read Toren's *My Drink* composition on an email attachment. I want to ask them what they think about Toren's pleas, the time he said he had hinted to them about his distress. But we're raw now. We can't talk about this yet. All of us are waiting for more information, waiting to examine ourselves more closely. And it looks like what Toren has set in motion will pull us right along with him. Toren's bravery and courage seem almost a miracle for our family, although I wouldn't have requested it. We're brewing up our own plans for rehab.

6

You're All in Denial

What the hell am I doing in rehab? I think I've always been a pretty level-headed guy, but I had a lot coming to me in my first days back from my halted venture in South America. Things had certainly changed since the good old days. Being a part of the student body at my university gave me license to party, get as messed up as I wanted—as long as I held up my end of the deal: get objective, measurable results that justified the absurd weekends that washed all that hearty education right out of my brain.

Who cares? I certainly didn't and there wasn't anyone else who would intervene because most of my drinking (scary enough) seemed normal, as long as you remember that any good drunk will surround himself with people who can party like a rock star as well. So what's the problem? I was a great student, from a great family and I became a damn good volunteer. And don't question my motives in South America because, by signing up, I wasn't avoiding my drinking, the real world, or the crap-ass job market. I entered the Peace Corps for other self-seeking reasons.

I've worked hard to paint such a bad-boy image of myself. I wasn't always this way. My decision to go into the Peace Corps stems from visions I'd had since I was young. I'd traveled with my family and experienced the beauty and cultural diversity offered in the world. As a child, I always dreamt of being a professional athlete, musician, and artist all in one lifetime—and a sensitive, fun-loving and adventuresome person, as well. I never envisioned I'd be the 'I Told You So' poster boy for the D.A.R.E. Program.

When it came time to start making post-college plans and

decisions, Peace Corps seemed like a worthy option. Although I realized I'd have to sacrifice countless familiarities, my sense of self, my passion for the music scene, and everything else that rocked about being young in 'the good old United States of America,' I felt I had a chance to learn another way of living, become a part of something bigger, and to potentially give a little something back to a life that had given me everything. I may have been able to maintain the course of my childhood dreams but, as a result of my drinking, all that I had ever envisioned hit the skids. Somewhere muddled up in my adolescence, 'alcohol' and 'ism' intermixed and my disease began to reveal itself.

So how did I land in rehab?

After being assessed by a professional in Washington, D.C., as a result of my desperate honesty (something new for me), I was told that I was an alcoholic and would need to go to an inpatient rehabilitation facility to learn about my disease and how to live with it. Screw that. Give me some therapy and some ways to deal with or control my drinking and put me on a plane back to South America. That's what I thought. With some tears and more compromise, I figured I'd hold up my end of the deal, and after I was out of rehab and the doctors found out how great I was and how different I was, they'd just send me back to my wonderful life down in hinterland. I am an exception, and always have been, right? DENIAL.

My first day in group therapy, I told everyone my story, what brought me to rehab, how I always drank to get drunk, and that I felt that my withdrawal symptoms were getting so bad and unbearable that I'd asked for help. I was okay because I had asked for help and knew something was wrong, right? I wasn't in denial. Besides, I looked around the place and saw all these crazy people with outrageous stories—addicts, lowlifes, winos—and I knew that I wasn't like them. I was fine. This center was full of people in pain, with damaged marriages or devastated families, pending charges and court orders, and all kinds of shame, guilt, and depression. These people were extremely sick.

When I was 'done' and had shared my story, I felt pretty good about my situation and my honesty. We switched to some other people in the group and talked about some of their drinking, old habits and behaviors, problems and so on. It was amazing how their denial completely disallowed them to see their own lives and drinking objectively and how their actions drastically affected other people. I thought it was insane. How could these guys not know that carting vodka into the office, drinking on the way home from rehab or a detox, countless DUIs or other offenses, or all the deterioration of their hobbies and personal relationships indicated that they were alcoholic, they had lost control, and that they were powerless over their substance? Their defenses were strong and they were in complete denial.

I wasn't in denial because I had asked for help and I came to rehab willingly. My story seemed so much better than most and so clear to me. Since my blackouts and withdrawals were worsening, I was tired of it. So I figured rehab was necessary for the proper adjustments. It felt good to finally talk about what had been bothering me for some time now and it was easy for me to describe what worried me about my drinking. I didn't have any shame, guilt or real consequences with my consumption. I drank purely as a recreation and whether I 'used' to 'escape,' well—who cares?

The point is, I was doing it with all my good friends and we seemed to be just where we wanted to be, all the time. Alcohol had really been a blessing to me and the fact that I was in rehab angered me a bit. I may have been able to use some help but this was lame. I was able to shrug it off as another 'part of my story' and thought it would be a good learning experience. I didn't realize that these observations would both be powerfully true.

"Hi, my name is Toren, and I'm an alcoholic." The first time I ever said that was in an AA meeting. I was nineteen and had just finished my freshman year of college. It really meant nothing to me in 1999. I said it with no ownership; I was there only because I was supposed to be. I said it because everyone else said it, but it didn't apply to me at the time. In 1999, at the end of my freshman year of college, my loving campus Residence Director (RD) told me that in order to be able to return to school the following fall, I would have to attend ten AA meetings and learn about the consequences of drinking and evaluate the seriousness of my problem. What the fuck did he know?

My freshman year was one big celebration in a bottle, can, pill, pipe or whatever seemed to fit or make itself available on that given Wednesday, Friday night, Sunday afternoon or what have you. College life was a great chance to capitalize on everything that I had begun to excel at by the end of high school: having fun and not adhering to the rules or circumstances that applied to everyone else.

My first night in the dorms before most people arrived, I unpacked and got settled in with blaring music and I guzzled down about seven or eight ice beers like any normal person would do. I was at home. Coincidentally, I was put in a dorm with a bunch of kids that shared my love for partying. In college? Go figure. We flourished in our new environment. But put a bunch of inventive college kids together and the outcome is almost a guarantee. I was in a single room and had no one to blame for all the behavioral issues that were to follow.

By week three or four, I had been written up three different times for alcohol violations and had several meetings with the RA (Residence Assistant) and RD (Residence Director). But screw them all. The rules were too strict; the RA's weren't fair and were going after or picking on certain people. I just had bad luck. I'd be damned if I was going to mellow out—this was college, for God's sake.

With some of my new buddies, I made frequent trips to a big grocery store and got kicks out of sneaking cheap handles of vodka, 40s and tall cans of malt liquor, and glorious half-racks of shitty ice beers into the dorms. Always giddy and excited, we exercised our freedom to celebrate or abuse every chance we got, and that was often. Excessive drinking led to plenty of random acts of chaos, the occasional trashcan fire or petty vandalism, or general insanity. It was all fun and games and no one got hurt. With more and more write-ups, and empties collecting outside our entryway, ours became a marked building. The unpredictable 'fire drills' that required the whole building to evacuate in the middle of the night were a joke to us. I guess no one else enjoyed it on as many levels as we did. The staff surely didn't. Attempting to control all of us seemed to make us wilder and more rebellious and we ate it up. It was an exciting time for a bunch of 'real students.'

My grades were outstanding that fall and my party achievements were, as well. But by spring, my standing on campus had gotten pretty ugly. I was a victim of unfair and unwanted attention by the campus police. After being 'relocated' away from most of my friends and moved up onto main campus, I was given fair warning. No more violations or setting foot on the lower portion of campus or I was out. Hmmm...what was going on? I had only bad things to say about all the rich and snooty people on the campus and the 'nothing-better-to-do' Public Safety Team. They patrolled past my door constantly and, on weekends, even checked the balcony with a spotlight in order to make sure there were no shenanigans happening after-hours. I was pretty fed up at this point with all these authority figures on their high horses telling me what to do and singling me out. I wasn't the only minor drinking, on or off campus, and I sure as hell didn't need my hand held in my adjustment to college life—my grades were fine.

I continued to push buttons, bend rules and enjoy my first year of college as I pleased. I managed to remain on campus, although barely, the entire year. While my grades were suffering a bit that spring, I was also working part-time for dining services setting up snacks and drink bars for big-money conferences and helping to cater special events on campus. The occasional complimentary wine was nice on the side of the weak-ass paychecks. In my last meeting with the RD, we had a serious chat. The cumulative behavior and damage was enough, I guess. He understood in some way that a lot of people have problems adjusting to college and that maybe it would be good for me to evaluate and check my motivation for being in school.

Well, that was a mistake. I was there to have fun, party and meet new people and, of course, to get that pricey degree—in four years or under. My parents were paying for my education, not for my exploitation of college life, and it was my job to perform in school in order to stay. I was walking a fine line and my parents were always on the other end with my mom's radar, questions and concerns and, thankfully, their support and unconditional love. It was tough to satisfy my expectations, my parents, and all those people catching my mistakes. No one from the college contacted my parents nor informed them what I'd been up to.

The RD told me that in order to return, there had to be some major changes in my attitude. My current behavior would not be allowed. What he couldn't understand was how I could be such a reasonable person yet be the same guy who got caught twice publicly urinating in the same spot—the second time out of drunken spite. Why was it like dealing with an angel in our face-to-face meetings and like dealing with the devil at night when confronted by public safety? My answer was simple: those bastards were always following us around, trying to catch or control us, and we just wanted to do what respectable college kids are doing everywhere. Therefore, I didn't like Public Safety and I let them know it at certain times.

Surprisingly, this brilliant answer didn't really cut it. I would not be allowed to live on campus the following year. The RD said it was a shame that sometimes some of the brightest kids with the most potential seemed to cause the most trouble and find themselves with the most problems. I thought it was a shame that he was a forty-year-old man living in the dorm babysitting a bunch of college kids and penalizing them for their basic right to have fun. We were completely justified in raging and spending our youth and invincibility while we had it. He also told me to go to those AA meetings. What a joker. He didn't know who I was.

7

BingeDrinking…bingedrinkn…
bingingdrunk..ing
bigdrunkmingblmgdg

Don't just give me a beer. I've never done one beer. Give me all
the beer.   Toren Volkmann, 2003

When our boys were adolescents, I posted a chart about binge
drinking in the bathroom. I was hoping that not only would the
brothers read it, but that all their friends who trooped in and out
of our house would notice it as well. It would advise that I was
aware of alcohol abuse and tip them off that they weren't concealing
drinking behaviors from me. It might cause them to think. It might
also cause them to avoid me, but it seemed worth the risk. The
chart, printed on sea-green paper, stated salient facts from an
American Medical Association survey. It defined binge drinking as
the consumption of five or more drinks in a row (four for women),
one or more times during a two week period; drinking to get drunk.
I talked with (or at) our boys about binging, and mostly they just
peered back at me. But at least I had done my job. I had dared to
bring it up.

The green-colored list still hangs in the bathroom when I check
for it after our conference call with Toren's addiction counselor Carl
in Washington, D.C. I see that the chart also points out that lifelong
patterns of alcohol abuse are established in high school and that 10
million American youth under the age of twenty-one drink alcohol.
It says that boys usually try alcohol for the first time at eleven years
old; the average age for American girls' first drink is thirteen. [5]
After Carl's sobering call, I untape the list and stick it inside a drawer

with some extra towels. It hasn't done any good anyway.

Drinking these days is full of glamour. It seems everyone does it. The industry targets its marketing to every one of us: it will make us beautiful in those long, slinky black velvet dresses; it will make us more healthy if we have a glass of wine with our evening meal; it will make us playful and boyish as we munch pizza with our friends while watching football games; it will heighten romance and lure intimacy. Drinking alcohol is a legal and socially acceptable activity. All we have to do, after all, is drink responsibly. There's no mention in the promotion that alcoholism is a progressive, addictive disease. Drinking alcohol is not presented as a dirty, dangerous activity in the same way as smoking cigarettes. A few stiff ones won't pollute the environment or burn out our lungs. Imbibing spirits has a sophisticated social history dating back through the centuries, with nomenclature and boorish wine-tasting sommelier traditions, *n'est-ce pas?* We caution our children to wait until they're *ready* for alcohol, say age twenty-one. Then we hold our breath as they crash through the starting gates. Some of them launch earlier than others.

Adults drinking alcohol is quite different from adolescents drinking alcohol (an adolescent is a person twelve to twenty years old). It takes five to ten years for some adults to become alcoholic from the time of the first drink. But because adolescent brains are at a different stage of growth, *it may take only five to fifteen months for them to become alcoholic once they begin drinking.* Parents can suddenly find their perfectly normal kid transformed into a robot controlled by the disease of alcoholism in less than a year's time. [6] The most recent research is showing that the adolescent brain is even *more* vulnerable to the neurotoxic effects of alcohol than the adult brain.[7] Drinking during the teen years may be especially damaging to the hippocampus, a brain region that is important for learning new information. The brain does not quit developing until a person is in his/her mid-twenties, and one of the last regions to mature is the frontal lobe area which is needed for making judgments and the ability to plan. The young brain appears to be highly susceptible to the effects of alcohol, especially on learning and memory function. Data indicates that people in their twenties who have been alcoholics as teens have smaller hippocampal volumes. These studies are just now becoming available and provide a strong warning against teen drinking.[8]

But remember, when you're young, you're indestructible! My son doesn't relate to that pathetic guy with grey stubble lying in the gutter at 2 a.m. That bum's old and scarred, someone who shouldn't have been drinking in the first place, someone who obviously couldn't control himself. My son knows he couldn't become such a hopeless loser.

Sometimes parents learn about the way kids party whether they like it or not. We accidentally landed at one of our oldest son's parties when he was a junior in college. Since we knew many of his guests, fellow soccer players, we strolled outside onto the deck to talk with them. There I saw a large funnel lurking in the shadows. And I knew that the kids had been binging. (It was the kind of funnel used to fill the gas tank of a lawn mower, one you'd commonly have in your garage. Kids use funnels to drink large quantities of alcohol as quickly as possible, as if in a competition.) The attendees were mostly over twenty-one years old, at a quiet private residence, and were breaking no laws. So what was my beef? Hadn't I ever been to college? I pulled my son aside and asked him why he had that funnel. Immediately I was 'Oh, Mom'd! out of the party. I could tell our son was very perturbed.

Through the ensuing years, I found myself removing all colors and sizes of funnels from our kids' car trunks as we unexpectedly opened them to pack or unpack for various events. They didn't argue with me because they knew if I saw a funnel, it would be confiscated. Don't any other parents find these? Why has no one ever talked about it? Other parents probably figure, just as I did, that this binge drinking is a passing phase, harmless and short lived. It is other parents' kids who binge drink, not our own.

Much of the data on binge drinking originates on college campuses; this is natural because the collegiate arena is ideal for adolescent studies. Even though research is oriented towards users on the campus, problems exist wherever youth are drinking. Many kids drink during high school (the average beginning age is 13.1 years) and continue drinking afterwards, college or not. Including all young people (not just college kids), more than 10 million current drinkers in the United States are between the ages of twelve and twenty. Of these young drinkers, 20 percent engage in binge drinking and 6 percent are heavy drinkers.[9] Nearly one in every five teenagers (16 percent) has experienced blackouts after which they could not remember what happened the previous evening.[10]

It is commonly assumed that youth with fewer opportunities are more at risk for drug and alcohol abuse and that their lifestyle may be more hazardous. Numerous persons think that more studious youth move on to college and thereby have the least tendency for addiction problems. *But it may not be true.* Our college campuses are breeding colonies for high level alcohol addiction and abuse. Maybe those youth who choose not to attend college are less in jeopardy. Or perhaps they, too, are binging at the rate of college youth. There do not yet appear to be studies comparing alcohol use of college youth versus other similar-aged youth.

One of our boys once arrived home from college sporting a contraption of valves, tubes, and funnels. It was aptly and affectionately named after some sort of prehistoric reptile, and I could see it was a tool used for beer bonging (like a funnel for binge drinking) at college parties. They called it the "Triceptatrough." It wasn't Toren who brought it home, but one of his older brothers. He was proud of the workmanship, how he and his buddies had invented it. I told him to get it out of the house and he did. The boys knew how I felt about beer bongs.

Even back in the 1960s, I sensed that binge drinking was bad. A guy I knew in college used to chug whole pitchers of beer after rugby matches. I didn't like it because I thought it discharged too much alcohol into the system too fast. That's why I had made a point to talk with our boys about binge drinking. Since then, I've found out that it's even *more* serious than I ever realized. I hate to think what I would have done with the Triceptatrough had I known what I know now! Statistics show that young people who binge drink may risk serious damage to their brains and memory loss later during adulthood. *For an adolescent, even binge drinking one single time can cause irreparable harm.*[11] Heavy drinking experiments at Duke University showed impaired activity to brain receptors which are responsible for memory and learning. Not only is there concern about the immediate effects of heavy, chronic drinking, but also concerns about the long lasting consequences of this abuse.[12]

Adolescents who binge drink may be more susceptible to neurobehavioral effects of alcohol than are adults. Approximately 14 million people in the United States—one in every thirteen adults—abuses alcohol or is alcoholic. Males are more alcohol dependent and experience more alcohol-related problems. The highest rates of problems are among young adults ages eighteen to twenty-nine.[13] Repeated drinking kills the cells in specific brain areas. People who quit drinking after many years of alcohol abuse may still have significant memory deficits. Even social drinkers who drink heavily on the weekends can acquire these deficits, as can young people in high school, college, and the young adult working world.[14]

In *My Drink,* Toren talks about not being able to remember chunks of time when drinking. What he is describing is a blackout. I had always thought if you were blacked out, you were totally on the floor, passed out. But no, I find in my research that *during an alcohol-induced blackout, a person can be conscious but form no memory of the event.* It is because the hippocampus, a deep part of the brain associated with memory, shuts down. Dr. Aaron White at Duke University Medical Center has researched this phenomenon.[15] He found that during blackouts students do all kinds of activities such as driving autos, vandalizing property, engaging in sex, or spending large amounts of money. And the next day, they have no memory of it. This is a warning sign of damage being done to the brain. Furthermore, blackouts are common even among non-alcoholics. In the College Alcohol Study, one out of every four students who drank reported having forgotten where they were or what they did while drinking during the school year. The incidence of blackout was 54 percent among frequent binge drinkers. The average alcohol intake of females who blacked out was five drinks per occasion while with males it was nine drinks per occasion.[16]

When Toren was first caught drinking in high school in 1995, we did not know that he had been binge drinking. After he was discovered by us, of course he confessed to drinking alcohol. But never did we parents know the extent. If we had, we should have been alarmed because *kids who binge drink are more likely to have problems with alcohol addiction further down the road.* Chances for a male becoming addicted to alcohol increase tremendously if he consumes more than three or four drinks per day. For females, it's about three drinks per day. Brain damage due to heavy drinking occurs sooner than scientists thought possible. Lab animals who were allowed to binge drink around the clock for four days showed immediate damage. According to the resource book *Buzzed* [17]:

Five areas of mental ability are compromised by chronic alcohol abuse (or binge drinking)—

1. **Memory formation**

   Kids become unable to form new memories. An individual will recall what he learned earlier in life, but not what he ate for lunch two hours ago.

2. **Abstract thinking**

   One way to measure abstract thinking is to show someone a group of objects and have her group the objects according to shared characteristics. Binge drinkers will consistently group things based on concrete characteristics (such as size, color, shape) rather than on abstract characteristics (such as what they are used for, what kinds of things they are).

3. **Problem Solving**

   Persons who are chronic drinkers often have difficulty here. They get stuck in one mode, take longer to find a solution. The executive functions of the frontal lobes appear damaged.

4. **Attention and Concentration**

   It is difficult for chronic drinkers to focus attention, especially visual attention (like reading an instruction manual).

5. **Perception of Emotion**

   It appears that binge drinkers have difficulty perceiving emotion in people's language, especially hearing the tone and cadence of language. This can cause difficulty in social relationships.

I cringe when I learn the damage caused to the brain by binge drinking, tissue that shrinks and dies and cannot be replaced, thinking my own son may now face these deficits. I read that the discrepancies may disappear as time passes, but there is evidence that even after seven years, many chronic drinkers retain significant memory deficits.

Binge drinking oftentimes begins in middle and high school, as Toren reports. Statistics say that if a student binges in high school, she will be three times as likely to binge in college. Over half the binge drinkers, almost one in four students, are frequent binge drinkers, that is, they binge three or more times in a two week period. (One in five students abstains from alcohol.)[18]

College presidents agree that *binge drinking is the most serious problem on campus.* So why aren't more parents talking about this? Is it because we send the kids away and don't have to watch what's happening? Why do we see news reports of drunken campus fiascos and it's always someone else's kids? If 40 percent of all students are binge drinkers according to the 1999 College Alcohol Survey, who is paying their tuition? (Don and I, times three).

When you really think about it, binge drinking seems like an odd thing to do, pouring vast quantities of specialty poison down your throat. It's especially strange for grown-ups to contemplate. Here's why kids binge drink: According to research, *both peer pressure and the status of drinking lend a jump-start to binge drinking.* [19] I try to figure out what influenced our boys so heavily. Certainly our kids viewed alcohol at parties hosted by Don and me, and perhaps they found the allure too enticing. Even though we did not consider our use of alcohol excessive as they were growing up, when we did consume it, we had the house decorated with candles and fine food, and we socialized with laughing and happy people. The image of alcohol as a necessary and fun party enhancer was certainly reinforced in our household, even though we didn't have funnels hooked onto our belt loops.

Literature about alcoholism maintains that people who are addicted to alcohol are often abusers of other substances. Nicotine, marijuana, cocaine, or even eating disorders are varieties of such addictions. Toren selected alcohol for his disease, but during his foray, he admits that he also experimented with other drugs and cigarettes. Although he abandoned them along the way, some alcoholics are unable to do this. Or perhaps when they kick alcohol, they turn to other addictions to replace it.

"The recurrence of binge drinking at the adolescent and college levels has reestablished the tradition of heavy drinking by our American ancestors. And, as a nation, we are consuming more alcohol each year." The book, *A Nation Under the Influence* [20], provides an excellent history and current analysis of alcohol use. Presently, alcohol reigns BIG in American Society. And it has been KING for years. My husband interned at Harlem Hospital in New York City in the 1970s, a time when everyone was concerned about heroin, dope (marijuana), cocaine, and later, crack. But what he saw was that alcohol was by far the most common cause of ruin, heartache and health problems, to the people he treated in New York. It hasn't changed all that much in his present day practice here in Olympia, Washington, thirty years later. Alcohol still drives medical and social problems seen by my husband's profession.

In the 1999 College Alcohol Survey, less that 1 percent of students reported using crack, heroin or LSD, and less than 2 percent used other barbiturates, and only about 5 percent reported using any illicit drugs ever. About 27 percent smoked marijuana and 29 percent smoked cigarettes. But 68 percent of students drank alcohol, and 44 percent binged. Even though alcohol washes over all other drug use on college campuses and causes more damage and expense, the federal government excludes alcohol from its blatant war on drugs. This exclusion exists because the alcohol industry lobbied for it, which reinforces the idea that alcohol is benign and further legitimizes (underage) alcohol abuse.[21]

Alcohol abuse causes not only devastation to the brain, but carries risks of cancer, liver and digestive failure, heart disease, problems with the pancreas, colon and esophagus, high blood pressure, not to mention social risks of divorce and domestic violence. With a history of ongoing alcohol-related problems such as these, you'd think there would have been enlightenment by now. People should begin to figure it out. But recent studies indicate that alcohol is *the* drug of choice by educated partiers. And they're serious about it. They continue to drink and drink, even when it causes death. In 2002, *The British Medical Journal* found that death rates for young adults and middle-aged women increased with the amount of alcohol they consumed, even as little as one drink per week.[22] Alcohol is the preferred legal tool for both intoxication and death. We just seem to love it to death. How could we blame our kids for loving it, too?

You'd think our Perfect Family did little to stop our alcohol-crazed children. But it's not true. We tried several ideas, one of which was using a Breathalyzer. The Breathalyzer idea came about after we'd dined out with some of our closest adult friends one night in Tacoma. Having finished three hours of reminiscing and dining, each couple would be driving to homes in Olympia and Seattle. Some of us had consumed martinis prior to dinner and all of us had drunk wine with dinner. Two people had cognac after dessert. One of my friends said she was to be the designated driver, because her husband had imbibed both martinis and cognac.

Upon arriving at our cars in the parking lot, one of the guys proposed that all of us blow on a Breathalyzer; he had just purchased one and it was inside his car. We were curious, so we all tried it out. To our consternation and surprise, several of us were over Washington State's 0.08 percent blood alcohol level, a legal definition of drunk, including the aforementioned designated driver (who had only consumed wine with her dinner). Her husband, on the other hand, was well below the limit, even with a martini, wine, and cognac. "It's because he ate bread," his wife insisted. As a result of our parking lot Breathalyzer test, we adjusted drivers and proceeded home. (Perhaps every car in America should come equipped with a Breathalyzer.)

After this, Don and I bought one as well, to use on ourselves and on our kids. More than once, it proved a reliable measure of consumption. We made use of it sporadically to test our boys when they returned home from social events. So along with the markings imprinted on our sons by the glorification and enhancement of alcohol, we were left to examine our own behaviors. When we said "Cheers!" as a toast before a meal or a social event, we needed to think what it meant, whether we were really at ease about our next sip.

In late September, after Toren's phone calls from Washington, D.C., our family had a quiet period of one week where we didn't hear from him because the first days of his addiction program did not allow outside contact. So I called his brothers. We talked frankly about binge drinking for the first time. Even though I'd posted the green list during their high school and college years, it had been *me* talking, not *them*. Now they were able to tell me about it more easily. Yes, there'd been binging. It's like tap water in college. Fraternities, sports teams, dorm buddies, apartment friends and sororities, almost everyone partied (except for the one in five who abstains.) Even kids who didn't attend college but lived on their own participated in binging. The boys didn't think it was necessarily a problem. Just something a young person needed to be aware of. And these brothers come from the same family as Toren, their binge drinking brother, who floundered into the pit of alcoholism. I'm trying to make sense of it; that crumpled list in the towel drawer.

A study from 2002 shows that 31 percent of college students meet clinical criteria for misuse of alcohol.[23] One in ten college men under age twenty-four meets the twelve-month diagnosis of alcohol dependence.

So our Toren fits into the one in ten. How could we have identified him sooner? There's the CAGE test, one developed by Dr. John Ewing. It goes like this:

✓ Have you ever felt you should **C**ut down on your drinking?
✓ Have people **A**nnoyed you by criticizing your drinking?
✓ Have you ever felt bad or **G**uilty about your drinking?
✓ Have you ever had a drink first thing in the morning to steady your nerves or to get rid of a hangover (**E**ye opener)?

CAGE is what it spells, and it indicates a possible alcohol problem.[24] With one "yes" it is possible that a problem exists; more than one, it is highly likely a problem exists.

As if our kids would have been honest with us about the CAGE questions! Or that they would have taken them seriously. And what's more, some studies have shown that females tend to feel guilty about drinking no matter how much they consume and frequently reply "yes" to the 'G' question. While the CAGE test is one tool, it may not be totally reliable. There are many other tests, among them one called TWEAK, one called MAST, and another called CUGE which bring forth differing results.

So, what's a binge drinker to do but keep on binging?

A college-aged binger is 21 times more likely to have:

- ✓ missed classes
- ✓ fallen behind in school work
- ✓ damaged property
- ✓ been hurt or injured
- ✓ engaged in unplanned sexual activity
- ✓ not used protection when having sex
- ✓ gotten in trouble with campus police
- ✓ driven a car after drinking [25]

Binge drinkers cause problems for other students as well as themselves by being intoxicated: arguing, assaulting, and insulting. With 47 percent of college students who consume alcohol drinking to get drunk, it means that American campuses are experiencing a myriad of social problems related to alcohol.

Evidently, my green list in the drawer was an insufficient education. And neither did the D.A.R.E. program offered by our schools seem to impact Toren's decisions. In fact, one of Toren's friends recently commented to me that it was the D.A.R.E. program that first informed him about, and heightened, his interest in substances. He did not feel it was an effective tool. (This program is typically taught to ten and eleven-year-old students in grades five and six by police officers. It aims to inform about alcohol and other drugs and to teach social and decision-making skills to help students resist their use.) Studies have found that D.A.R.E. essentially has no impact on alcohol use.[26]

So in lieu of successful alcohol education, clever media ads and peer influence have triumphed. The more I learn about the behavior of binge drinkers and the effects of this national pastime, the more thankful I am that Toren was able to graduate and move on. Because the marinade of a binge drinker is delivered by the funnelful.

8

I Don't Give a Rat's Ass

Getting into trouble on campus wasn't my fault. Throughout most of my freshman year of college, I continued to do things my way. I managed to shrug off monetary fines and attributed the various unreasonable punitive measures to external forces and the stupidity of a system developed by a bunch of people who couldn't take a joke. Besides, it wasn't reality; it was a little happy bubble of a campus. In the real world, I would blend in better.

I was extremely good at seeing the faults of others and pointing out anyone who wasn't conducive to my path of self destruction. I was also real successful at twisting a story to justify the outcome and consequences of my behavior. "No, Mom and Dad, you see—this happened, that happened, and then THEY did this—or actually..." In reality, I was just trying to protect them and myself. I wasn't proud of some of the things that happened. But I wasn't necessarily ashamed, either. Still, I could never let my parents know that my first year away at school was defined by chaos, crazy consumption of alcohol and disregard for anyone in the way of my fun. One long binge, more or less. What an awesome year.

I went to two AA meetings out of the required ten the summer after my freshman year, and I realized two things:

1. That AA wasn't for me.
2. That the folks who mandated it would never find out that I didn't actually go to ten meetings.

I was right about the latter.

I told my parents that I went to the meetings for a class—over the summer? They had damn well better believe it. I was a psychology major, and besides, my poisoned mind was beginning to believe some of the things I told them as well as some of the things I told myself. I was choosing to live off campus because, well, because it was closer. To what? The liquor store, I guess. Either way, I was very careful only to let some of the truth show— enough only for my parents to get the idea that there was an occasional brush with the law or an incident with the campus police, and that it was just another learning experience for their sparkling little college-going boy.

During the fall of 2000, I gained prospects for learning experiences while studying abroad on the Semester at Sea Program. I put a lot of work into getting the 'nod of approval' from my parents and worked hard to stay out of trouble so I could set sail without losing the chance beforehand.

This voyage of discovery embarked from Vancouver, B.C., first docking in Japan, then continuing south and west through China, India, Africa, South America and, eventually, through Cuba and home. I realized that this circumnavigation of the globe was an incredible opportunity and I made it my goal to complete it without any unwanted infractions, tickets, visits to *cárceles* (jails) or dangerous situations.

Aboard ship, alcohol was served nightly (during limited hours) and numerous occasions arose for drinking—on and offshore. At the beginning, I tried to stay out of the alcohol scene for many reasons, but as I learned to know people, I slowly came into my own as the lush that I normally was. I didn't have any severe withdrawal symptoms at this point and, for the most part, my extra precautionary measures kept me out of trouble in port cities.

By the end of the semester-long voyage, I'd say I was drinking heavily but had not joined the club of notorious drinkers banned from ANY alcohol on or off the ship. (Enough problems with alcohol arose for certain people that they were forced to attend meetings and were no longer allowed the privilege to consume alcohol at the threat of being sent home.) I somehow slid under that radar despite plenty of heavy drinking which increased as I became comfortable with the people, the ship, and the constant change of locales. I got 'caught' extremely intoxicated onboard one time and was issued a warning for the infraction, but nothing serious happened. In the last few port cities, I began taking risks and had some solid blackouts, but experienced no alarming consequences.

Well...we returned stateside in late December and, sometime after the New Year, I received a Christmas card in the mail printed with something very generic, like 'Happy Holidays,' and below someone had written, "*Hey Toren, I don't know if you remember me, but I helped you back to the ship the last night in Cuba. I hope you are well. Seasons Greetings and take care.*"

No. I didn't know who it was. I could not recall the student whose name I saw signed on the note. (And after looking through several books of student pictures, I still don't know.) I felt horrified, embarrassed, and confused when I received the greeting. I'm not even sure if I *knew* I had blacked out, as a matter of fact. I never responded and eventually threw the card away because it was an irritating reminder that I couldn't remember squat and I didn't know who had helped me. So I guess I didn't have any 'incidents' at sea but I just barely floated by.

My living situation during college years continued to fluctuate. After all the problems I caused on campus my freshman year, I disappeared sophomore year, living off campus in an apartment, followed by my studies abroad with Semester at Sea. This time lapse seemed to be sufficient because when I returned the second semester of my junior year, I was allowed to live on campus. During this period I managed to navigate between the cracks with very little trouble and only a few visits from the public safety officers. It wasn't until the last month of my senior year that I had my final run-in with the head RD.

Allegations of a broken car window lead straight back to me after a long weekend and a wild party. Some things were 'allegedly' thrown from our third story balcony. I stepped forward and took the blame I deserved when I realized enough evidence had piled up against me. I ended up funding the windshield replacement. The RD didn't know which question to ask first: "How is it that you are living on campus?" and "How have I not known about it?" and "How have you been staying out of trouble?" and finally, "What happened here?" After we got past all this, he made me promise that no more problems would occur, considering I wasn't even technically allowed to live on campus, and that I was so close to graduating and moving on. I had almost made it, and I think that idea thrilled him as much (or more so) than me. He attended graduation and the moment finally came where I 'walked' and he knew that it was over. I think we were both pretty pleased.

One reason I didn't get into much trouble on campus my senior year was because I spent a good part of the weekends in 2002 off-campus, partying elsewhere. I may have been getting ready to join the real world, but my alcoholism was progressing rapidly at this point and affecting my studies dramatically.

In hopes of better preparing myself for graduate school and to get a taste of something more specific in the field of psychology, I had the opportunity to assist with research at one of the nearby state schools. The final semester of college, I worked two or three times a week at another campus in the Behavioral Teratology Department. The research specifically investigated exposure of newborn rats to alcohol and nicotine and measured its effects on the rats' behaviors and learning capacities.

Using rats as models (given that the rats' first weeks of life are similar to the last trimester of prenatal development during human pregnancy), the research studied how exposure to alcohol or nicotine impaired physical development in the brain and central nervous system as well as behaviorally in regard to learning. The research also looked at differences in severity between levels of exposure and duration while attempting to discover if there were any treatments that could be administered to abate or counteract fetal alcohol damage. I observed how the studies were designed and run, helped out entering data, and ran some of the very basic pilot studies being developed for future research. It all sounds routine, but it was a bit more difficult than it appears. Watch out, the irony gets thick.

The rats' abilities to learn were measured through behavioral tests such as swimming, climbing, and navigating mazes, while other tests measured the regularity or irregularity of their movements in a box designed to quantify such activity. It was hypothesized that rats exposed to various given levels of alcohol would perform differently and demonstrate less learning aptitude and, therefore, less improvement from previous testing.

I usually worked on Mondays, Wednesdays and Fridays. Interestingly, I found that *I* was able to perform *my* tasks better on Wednesday and Friday depending on how much alcohol *I* had exposed *myself* to on the previous weekend. (A number of Mondays I had not even made it home to campus before going straight to my 'internship'—to begin my always difficult Monday, usually feeling sick, feverish and bracing for withdrawals.) Meanwhile, I learned that some research indicates that one of the most damaging contributors to the rats' development is the withdrawal period. In fact, our research lab attempted to find substances to administer to the rats to lessen the damaging effects of withdrawal. It was hoped that this substance could one day be administered to human females who drank heavily during pregnancy in order to alleviate retardation, fetal alcohol syndrome, and other adverse consequences of alcohol, nicotine, or other chemicals. These substances damage the development of the fetus and affect behaviors involved with learning (prenatal damage by teratogens).

At various times, it was my job to select certain rats—all in labeled cages—to number them individually, then measure their movement and activity in one of three or four different boxes. I would have four boxes going at once, with three or four rats already numbered and waiting in each of the four cages until all of them had been processed. The rats would be tested for a specific time and for a certain amount of sequential days, always under identical conditions. This procedure was tricky and became confusing because I often tried to accomplish the detailed methodology in a screwed-up state of mind; I felt like I was experiencing worse withdrawal symptoms than the alcohol-saturated lab rats.

I dreaded going to work at the lab, especially on Mondays, because the ideas underlying our research were being rubbed in my face. It was obvious that my memory was failing as a direct result of my drinking. The timing of it proved exquisite. Still, I was not willing to acknowledge my drinking problem. My own alcohol consumption did not allow me to effectively contribute to academic research, which was attempting to tackle the root of *my* problem— abuse of alcohol. I refused to let this knowledge stop my self-destruction, even though it revealed to me the effects of my drinking on a scary level. At times, I was a wreck and I messed up a few of the procedures, testing the wrong subject in the wrong box, or mixing certain rats back into the wrong cages overnight between tests. (It turns out that the rats' reproductive systems didn't seem to be too affected; males and females were not supposed to be mixed. Oops.)

"Hi my name is Toren; I'm an alcoholic." This time when I said it, the fall of 2003, I was twenty-four and in rehab, so it was a little bit different. But still, I was saying it as a way of taking the path of least resistance. I didn't want to challenge the idea because that would require me to examine the problem and see why I was really there. As it turns out, I didn't know what being an alcoholic meant. I knew general stuff and knew that it carried a bunch of colorful stigmas but it was always one of those things you heard about and, unless it directly affected you, you could pass through life ignoring it.

Actually, I have found out that you can be an alcoholic and still discount it. Being in rehab, seeing other examples, man, you can learn to ignore it; you can stay in denial until it drags you to your grave and devastates everything in your path.

But I was an expert on my drinking and didn't see what there was to be fixed in my therapy. In this particular rehab, each patient is given a specific treatment plan and requested to take steps in understanding his addiction and the disease, how it has affected him and his loved ones and what he needs to do in order to get control of his life to escape a horrible physical, mental, and spiritual deterioration. Sounds pretty deep for a rehab, huh? Well, it is.

For me, I thought it'd be easy. I wasn't really an addict. I'd only craved alcohol more recently, and that was only when I'd started in drinking already. I didn't drink daily, and sobriety was good to me when I needed to be sober. Shit, I didn't have a disease. I *chose* to drink and party in high school and college, and it was always great for me. My use didn't affect anyone else. Most people had no idea how much I drank, and when I blacked out I wasn't losing their memory, only mine. And finally, I had control over my life—well, for the most part, anyway.

9

Dysfunctional R Us?

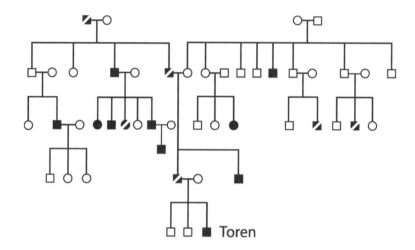

24 September 2003. As soon as Don and I find out the name of the rehab facility where Toren is assigned, we jump onto the Internet. The site looks encouraging and upbeat. I suddenly have hope. Toren's rehabilitation program offers more information about alcohol and drug addiction than I can comprehend. Definitions, charts, slide shows, resources, photos of staff and grounds, philosophy, the 'contact us' portion—it's all there. But this friendly site purports the Dysfunctional Family Label as a cause of an adolescent's demise. "The family is being neglected," the slide show states. It goes on to say how families aren't sitting down to dinner together anymore, how families lack control and structure. It emphasizes that family education is a tool of recovery. I agree that some families are

dysfunctional. But I differ about ours.

To me, the cause for the Perfect Family's dilemma is elusive. Yet everywhere we look, fingers point and the world screams back: Dysfunctional!! I put on my armor and rush out to combat this hated misnomer. How dare they name-call in our direction! This mother is ready to ride into battle. Maybe I need something to get mad at. I'm weary of being so damned understanding and loving. It's time to bring out my defensive reinforcements.

Let's start with sitting down as a family for dinner. If you challenged any one of our sons about the Volkmann dinner hour, they would laugh in your face. We sat down at six o'clock whether anyone wanted to or not. And dinner was not only nutritious and plentiful, but made from scratch. Enough said.

And as for structure, well there again, the boys would ridicule this premise right off the website. Who was known as the strictest mother in middle school? Probably me. Perhaps…just maybe, this is what drove my son to drink.

"So get over it," my husband says. "Just because you consider yourself the perfect mother, doesn't mean you have the perfect son."

Believe me, many fine drunks are nurtured in families who sit down jointly for dinner every night, read excellent literature together, make and enforce strict ground rules, and emphasize ethics and morals. In fact, the quality of alcoholics produced in such a family is outstanding. I'm here to prove it. (Actual results may vary).

Let's find another category to dis this Perfect Family. We're laying out all the reasons for an alcoholic's downfall and, as yet, we've skipped a vital category: Genetics. Hello deep and scary skeletons of the Volkmann past. And greetings to the fanatical Shamberger DNA pool. I usually tell people that the defects of our family fall to my husband's side. It isn't really true, but it equalizes the sting of the dysfunctional dinner time accusation. I feel better already.

It's a statistical reality that if a person has a close relative (like parent, grandparent or aunt/uncle) who is an alcoholic, he has four times the chance of becoming an alcoholic. According to the NIAAA (National Institute on Alcohol Abuse and Alcoholism), researchers have uncovered a genetic factor that could predispose certain youths to binge drink.[27] College students with a particular variant of the serotonin transporter gene (5-HTT) drink more alcohol per occasion, drink more often just to get drunk, and are more likely to engage in binge drinking than students without the variant. This new evidence provides important research about the risk of developing a mal-adaptive pattern of alcohol consumption influenced by genetics.[28]

On my desk sits a stack of brochures and papers from the rehab institute. We have to fill out a form requested by Toren's therapist, Gretchen. She has such a Gestalt-sounding name; I know she will straighten him out. Gretchen has sent us a big packet of papers telling us about the twenty-eight day program, the Family Education Weekend, and she asks that we fill in data about our family alcohol history. It's called a Family Assessment, which sounds scary. I don't know if I want to send this private stuff across the country to be scrutinized by complete strangers. But then I remember we're desperate. Our son is in crisis. He's asking for help. I don't have to cover up for him now, because he's totally admitted he messed up. What a relief. Even though, as I said before and totally believe, he *is* a fabulous person with amazing qualities. We really raised him beautifully. There are just a few things in the way. Though I jest about this, I'm smarting on the inside. This isn't just a survey to summarize our family hobbies or avocations. It's a serious confession about the way we raised our son, about our values and family experiences, and we are requested to spell out the exact times where we fell short. I have to be honest.

The form mostly focuses on Toren's history (as I perceive it, which most likely could be, and is, different than how he perceives it). It asks what chemicals I think Toren is using or has used, when he started, and any negative behaviors I have encountered concerning his chemical use. It sounds pretty benign until I start listing nine years of drinking consequences on four inches of paper. There's hardly sufficient room. I become sweaty. Should I lie? Maybe delete a few screw-ups? I don't. I'm a Perfect Mother, remember? I write it as I saw it. And it hurts.

The assessment also asks about each family member's usage of

drugs and alcohol, like what drugs, how much, how often. I begin
to feel guilty when I have to write the word 'dope'—but they call it
'weed' now—and I can't remember how to spell 'marijuana.' There
are a lot of reasons I'm slowing down on my responses, because all
the sudden I'm thinking about thirty years ago. At that time I had
no idea this rehab center would be asking me these questions. You
don't think of that sort of thing in your twenties. You just do it. As
I think back on it, we didn't use marijuana that often; only for a
few years in the seventies. You can't complete medical school, an
internship, two different residencies, teach a classroom, play in a
symphony, and be three times pregnant and nursing while stoned
on marijuana. It won't work. Earning a living and being productive
was always a higher priority for Don and me, as well as carrying
and nourishing my babies drug and alcohol free. And it was scary
to buy an illegal substance. Even though we wore tie dyed shirts and
bell bottoms, we were lightweights. But I still feel a twinge of guilt
as I fill in the form. It whispers to me, "No wonder your son's in
trouble...."

On the next part of the questionnaire, our alcohol consumption
falls into the heavier than normal category, I speculate. I'm starting
to become more aware of this as we are not drinking during Toren's
treatment. It sticks out and now I realize we could cut back. So I fill
in that portion, too.

The next section asks about our families' generational
alcoholism/drug usage. There is about a half inch allowed for the
response. That's easy. My family has been Anabaptist, pacifist, and
non-drinking for generations. It would have been impossible to have
an alcoholic there. (Luckily the document doesn't ask for other
addictions, such as shopping, marathon running or Bible reading.)
But now Don is home and hands me a letter he has written to Toren. I
realize immediately that now we're going to need several attached pages.
As I said, it's *his* side of the family. Here's how Don describes it:

Hi Toren,
    The other day I was reading one doc's discussion on the
causes of alcoholism. His opinion is that 60 percent is genetic

and 40 percent environmental. I know this is hotly debated and you are learning all about that now. Regardless, you figured it out and that is what is saving you. Congratulations!

But just to give you a better understanding of your genetic background for whatever it may mean to you I will recount some of my family's history of alcoholism.

The Volkmann Hall of Alcoholics
(Those we know)

NANA'S SIDE ALCOHOLICS:

Two of Nana's brothers, Bert and Greg—She had six and they were all terribly colorblind, so they probably didn't even know if they were drinking light rum or dark rum and I am sure they didn't care, especially Greg. Bert, I think, conquered it okay. Greg died miserably from it, leaving a few pissed-off wives, but one sober kid.

Nana's sister's daughter, Beth (my first cousin)—She has been through lots and possibly more than one rehab program. She has turned her life around more than once, if you know what I mean. Nearly four years ago, in her late 40s, she apparently turned her life around again and, in fact, has been sober since. She's instrumental in counseling and supporting other alcoholics.

VOLKMANN SIDE ALCOHOLICS:

Great Granddad Tom—For his times, your Great Granddad had a bit of a wild streak. There were rumors of cases of Old Crow in the cellar. And he was known to fall asleep on the back of his wagon after a time in town. Fortunately, his sober horses were more on the wagon than was he and always returned him home safely.

Granddad's younger brother, Bill—Abandoned Lutheranism for Catholicism to marry wife Jane (an alcoholic). Bill died twenty some years ago from diabetes and other complications of life-long alcohol poisoning. Some considered him a closet drinker. It appeared to me that the *whole world was his closet.*

Bill & Jane's oldest daughter, Kathy *(my first cousin)—followed both her parents' alcoholic habits. Kathy's mother's family history (my Aunt Jane) is littered with stories of rehab attempts and alcoholic tragedy nearly too much to recount. Alcohol conquered Kathy at age 48 after a life-long battle. She died of cirrhosis and bleeding to death from a predictable complication of her destroyed liver.*

Bill & Jane's son, Grant *(my first cousin who took over his dad's orchard and bad habits)—He was the first person I knew who installed a keg in a refrigerator with the tap out the side! Yeah, baby! To his credit, he is nearly ten years sober now after losing one marriage to the disease. His son, Todd (in his twenties) has already been through a rehab program.*

Bill & Jane's three other children *(my first cousin)—As far as I know, two of these three siblings also may have had problems with addiction.*

Granddad's older brother Glenn's son, Tim *(my first cousin)—I remember him commenting several years ago, "I don't drink." I found out he recently celebrated fourteen years of sobriety. Prior to sobering up, he helped union workers deal with alcohol-related problems by getting them into rehab so they could return to their jobs. One day he realized that he was drinking more than those he tried to help, so he signed himself up for a program. He would be a good resource for you if you wish to talk with another family member.*

Granddad—*Has admitted to drinking way too much when in the military (what else could you do?) in his thirties. He has never had a "problem" and handles his "beer time" successfully for an 88 year old.*

My brother, your Uncle Ric—*He started drinking at an even earlier age than you, and smoking, and then doing drugs of all sorts. But, ultimately, alcohol was his favorite, although any 'high' probably worked. They say that he died* of snorting heroin, probably combined with too much alcohol—two huge depressants. He stopped breathing. Ric's typical 'booze-binge alone' or the 'heroin alone' would probably not have done him in that night, but at age 31 and with his history, it's hard to imagine anything but a tragic end to his life. According to those who were close to him at the time (I was just starting to get to know him better) he was in the process of 'cleaning up his act.' I would think cleaning up the Hanford Nuclear Site would have been easier.

Your Dad, me—Although I am not admitting to being an alcoholic (yet), I have not ruled it out. As a seven year old, I would pop open beer bottles for my dad and take a swig, but didn't like it. Never drank in high school except for one time. I didn't drink again until my freshman year in college where, after Hell Week in our fraternity (halfway through my freshman year). I had a sip of beer just because 85 people were about to kill me if I didn't (most of them are probably alcoholics). Slowly through college, I learned to drink a bit, occasionally getting drunk. Did some weed. The next few years, the same, sometimes overdoing it, but pretty controlled. Nothing regular. Never affected studies. Then med school, residencies, practice, the same.

A master of 'titration' I became. Both with the anesthetic drugs I administered to my patients and the booze that slithered down my throat. The past ten-plus years, having a drink after work and wine with dinner became a routine. Your mom and I have frequently talked about drinking less. So we made the rule: no weekday drinking and, of course, the unspoken 5 o'clock rule. Well, unless friends came over or there was another event, etc. And summer—one long weekend. Geez, sounds worse when I write it down. There have been some bad day-afters, feeling some hangover and a little shaky for an hour or so, making me think that it probably wasn't healthy. I have not had really bad reactions or trouble sleeping. I have looked forward to the weekend drink but have not felt a 'craving' exactly. It has never affected *my work, but I can recall twice going to work thinking that I wish I didn't feel the way I did.*

Probably ten years ago, your grandma said she was concerned that I was drinking more than I should. She asked, "When was the last time you went a week without drinking?" I informed her that I was on call lots so it had occurred. She was reassured. I was left wondering.

Today marks one week for me without drinking. I don't remember when that last happened. So, how am I doing after a week? Well, frankly, I missed having a drink out on the boat last evening and wonder how severe I need to be with myself. I don't want to give up drinking. But I don't want it to be a focus, a 'need,' a crutch or a problem. I will not be drinking for the duration of your program and will be assessing my situation throughout that time. After that, I will see how I feel and decide if I should moderate or quit.

So, Toren, that's one hell of a 60 percent for you to deal with. I thought you would want to know where you fit into the Family Hall. I'm counting on you being on the side with the happy, successful survivors. You can forever be an inspiration to the rest of our poor, genetically-challenged family members, like me. Thanks for helping me look at me.

Love,

Your Dad

Don's letter reveals a cumbersome appendage to our Perfect Family, one that neither of us had previously acknowledged. Nor had we ever really sat down with our children and discussed it. His data makes my green-colored binge drinking chart look anemic. I realize that we totally missed the boat here. Our kids needed to know this important family history and we slipped up by not forewarning them.

When Toren went to Mexico to study Spanish, he arrived shortly before *Día de los Muertos*, the Celebration of the Dead. It is a colorful fiesta to honor deceased family members. *Día de los Muertos* has a purpose. The Mexicans understand that there's a reason to celebrate with ancestors, to know them, to remember how they were. Our relatives' lives may help us recognize ourselves. Too often, we Americans just set them aside (a memorial service and a burial and *voilà*!) without understanding the impact. The history of our ancestors will, in fact, become our legacy, and we will carry parts of them forward with us. Sometimes unwillingly. All the better to know what we've got.

Toren will receive his father's letter at rehab, and we will also mail a copy to Gretchen, his therapist. Don and I failed to recognize the predisposition of our children to alcoholism. Now we have a crisis in our family, an addiction to be dealt with, whatever the cause. I find myself demoralized thinking about Toren's recovery from alcoholism, a disease that seems even more complicated than I thought.

We receive email correspondence from a fellow Peace Corps volunteer in South America, a person we've never met before, one who is enthusiastic about having Toren return to his post there. She suggests people we might contact to help Toren's cause. I write back that I cannot interfere with the decisions being made. In my heart, I'm thinking that Toren is not yet ready to decide whether he should return. While I'm gratified that this fellow volunteer feels Toren's work was of high quality, pushing him back up the hill will not help any of us. Maybe I, too, am moving along, because I now realize that protecting Toren will no longer serve him. His life is his own to create. I recall the term, 'codependent,' so I toss out to her that I don't want to be a codependent. It sounds knowledgeable, though I'm not exactly sure what it means. I seem to remember that being a codependent is not a good thing. All this addiction talk is new to me. I make a mental note to look it up.

I remember how my husband and I once placed M&Ms along the trail during Toren's first family backpacking trips. The candy encouraged him to continue on; it kept him content. And it made the hike easier for us. How young are patterns of codependency fostered?

No matter how we're labeled, we are a family bound by our love for one another. We function now as five grown people, separate, yet attached by years spent learning from one another. Some of our tendencies reach behind awareness, to places our grandparents traveled. Even though we weren't there, we know about it. Who said we are dysfunctional? Our Perfect Family swills success as it kneels down for a deserved smack in the head.

10

Start of (which?) God's Nightmare

Luck

I was nine years old.
I had been around liquor
all my life. My friends
drank too, but they could handle it.
We'd take cigarettes, beer,
a couple of girls
and go out to the fort.
We'd act silly.
Sometimes you'd pretend
to pass out so the girls
could examine you.
They'd put their hands
down your pants while
you lay there trying
not to laugh, or else
they would lean back,
close their eyes, and
let you feel them all over.
Once at a party my dad
came to the back porch
to take a leak.
We could hear voices
over the record player,
see people standing around
laughing and drinking.
When my dad finished

He zipped up, stared a while
at the starry sky—it was
always starry then
on summer nights—
and went back inside.
The girls had to go home.
I slept all night in the fort
with my best friend.
We kissed on the lips
and touched each other.
I saw the stars fade
toward morning.
I saw a woman sleeping
on our lawn.
I looked up her dress,
then I had a beer
and a cigarette.
Friends, I thought this
was living.
Indoors, someone
had put out a cigarette
in a jar of mustard.
I had a straight shot
from the bottle, then
a drink of warm Collins mix,
then another whisky.
And though I went from room
to room, no one was home.
What luck, I thought.
Years later,
I still wanted to give up
friends, love, starry skies,
for a house where no one
was home, no one coming back,
and all I could drink.

Raymond Carver, *All of Us* [29]

Toren built a fort during his high school days. He and a couple
of friends constructed it on the vacant lot across from our house. It

was nestled amidst cedar and fir trees, well-designed, and the boys even used a blueprint drawing. Because we thought they might be partying there, we forced them to tear it down. We told Toren it was his good luck to have parents who cared. He said it didn't seem like luck to him.

Toren gave us the sense that he wasn't lucky at all. He said he always got caught. We believed him at the time, but now I realize it wasn't the truth at all. The amount of times we caught him was miniscule. When we didn't catch him, sometimes someone else did. During his freshman year of high school, Toren attended a party (without our permission) at a river not far from our house, one of those situations you read about in the newspapers where someone drowns from drinking too much. But that didn't happen. Instead he got busted by the police (along with other more inexperienced kids who couldn't run fast enough or were also "unlucky.") One of his brothers was with him and also got caught. Toren swore to us it was his first high school party with alcohol and that he had not been drinking, just attending. But we decided to hand him a tough sentence. We penalized both Toren and his brother. They also had to go through legal steps for kids with MIPs (minor in possession). They were required to do community service.

Still in our files is the list of consequences we levied (each son had his own list):

Toren's Consequences:

Toren is a high school freshman, has a 3.79 accum. GPA, is a select year-around soccer player, lettered in swimming and started on the JV soccer team.

Toren's Penalties from April 16 to May 16, 1995:

1. Toren removed from high school JV soccer team.
2. Write letter of apology to asst. principal and high school soccer coach.
3. No going out for *one month*. Come straight home from school. No friends over.
4. No phone calls the first weekend. Afterwards, no phone calls after 8 p.m. for one month.
5. Urinalysis drug screen at local laboratory, 4/18/95. (*Negative results*)

6. Give away Nintendo. Out of house until further notice, perhaps forever.
7. Work out at community athletic club one hour per day.
8. Maximum 2 hours of TV per week, 2 hours per weekend.
9. Improvement of attitude to be measured at end of one month. Keep room picked up, take care of lawns, extra household chores each weekend. (painting, weeding, upkeep)
10. Visit grandparents out of town with family one weekend.
11. Spend evening with all house guests, visiting at dinner table, etc.
12. Loss of prized Beastie Boys tickets for 5/29/95. Not allowed to attend concert.
13. Community service:
   ✓ Crop Walk, collect $25
   ✓ 3 hours work at Neighborhood Beach
   ✓ Arrange to assist coaching throughout summer in youth soccer league (to begin first of June, several nights/week through August)
14. Meeting with parents of other boys involved in episode. Common ground rules set, information exchanged, phone numbers exchanged. Agreement to mutually support one another and one another's sons. (At this meeting, one set of parents advised me that we shouldn't be too hard on our boys, that they were just kids.)

Toren's guidelines from May 16 until end of summer:
1. Allowed to go out one night per weekend until 11 p.m., midnight if arranged ahead.
2. Limited viewing of TV: one program per night except Wednesdays.
3. Anticipation of all As and one Pass in college prep courses for grades in June 1995.
4. Part time summer job at cessation of school; save 3/4 of earnings for college.
5. Assist on soccer team, (community service).
6. Mow lawn every week.
7. Pay any increases in car insurance and/or court costs out of own funds.
8. Announce whereabouts to parents when leaving house.

There were about fifteen boys netted in that swoop. The above consequences established us as the strictest parents in the area. We didn't care because we felt it important to take a swift and immediate stand in regards to underage drinking.

This was the first time Toren was kicked off a high school sports team due to violating high school policy. But not the last. If you could joke about it, Toren turned out for three different varsity sports each year during high school; did that not increase the odds? It seemed that each season he was kicked off one or another team in accordance with the high school's alcohol and smoking no-tolerance rule.

Both Don and I worked closely with the coaches and parent groups at the high school. We had a good rapport with them. When we went to conferences about Toren's transgressions, all of us felt extremely chagrined. Late in Toren's high school career, one of Toren's best friend's mother would call to forewarn me to put on my power scarf and my power lipstick, because she and I were frequently called to attend these unpleasant debriefings together. We hoped Toren would 'get it' soon. It bothered me that Toren apologized so readily, spoke to us sincerely about his missteps, performed his penalties, and yet would make repeated infractions. Each time, we thought Toren had finally wised up.

As I thought I remembered, Toren did well with his penalties. In fact, it wasn't until Toren's rehab that I put two and two together, figuring out that HE DID *NOT* DO WELL. Not at all. I had to go back to my 1995 journal to dredge up the next incident. Surprisingly, the next event occurred just a few months after the river episode, subsequent to the severe restrictions we had thought would be so effective. And even more revealing is how much I had forgotten or minimized the experience. The next story has more details than I remember, but only because I wrote them down in my journal. I will relay the story as I interpreted it then, nine years before Toren would be enrolled in rehab. Little did I know that my rhetorical beginning would ultimately personify itself.

16 July 1995—Chris' Journal Entry

The power of helplessness. It can overtake. Knowing that all you've done for fifteen years wasn't enough preparation for a few hours of bad decisions. And knowing there remains a whole lifetime to do more damage, more destruction to oneself. That is helplessness. Many parents face it and give up. You think adolescence is the time of life to let go of your child, to allow the young person to turn the corner and carry his own weight. Ultimately, he'll bring along a sound mind and body, one that could function well in the world. Or the dreaded opposite, he will carry wreckage and damaged goods. A few hours can undo all the love and nurturing a parent has offered. Totally. It leads one to believe in helplessness. And that's where we are.

It began when Don and I were returning home from Seattle after attending a chamber music concert, an evening of Mozart and Schumann. We spotted Toren walking along North Street holding hands with a waify girl, accompanied by someone on a bicycle at 11:30 p.m. (Summer curfew at midnight.) I suggested we go over and let Toren know we were back, make sure he'd be in on time. Don said, "Let him be. It looks innocent enough." So we drove on home without bothering him.

At 12:10 a.m. he still wasn't in. His oldest brother had come in and gone to bed. It was a Wednesday night; both the older brothers had to get up by 6:30 a.m. for their summer jobs the next day. The second brother would be in by 12:30.

I checked downstairs and thought it smelled like someone had smoked a cigarette, but found no evidence of partying. Then I went to our back entrance where I found Toren "resting" on our landscaped hillside, the approach to our daylight basement. I called, "Toren, get in here!" and he said okay. He came upstairs into the great room, tripping as he entered. For a fifteen-year-old, stumbling is not highly unusual. But I watched him closely. He sprawled across the couch when I asked him to sit down, almost flopping. "Where have you been?"

He looked at me, glazed, and began mumbling things like, "We were walked then together mubuymumble." He stopped.

"What?"

"The others. We walked." He drooled.

"Oh, my God." I ran to get Don who was in bed watching TV, looking like he was about ready to fall asleep. "Don, Toren can hardly talk or walk. Get up here!"

He hurried along with me and had Toren stand up. "What have you had? Were you sniffing something? Drinking?" he asked in his ER triage voice.

Toren didn't make sense—he sputtered meaningless words until he garbled something like, "I've never drunk before. The first time."

"Where's your bicycle?" I asked him. I knew it was at the neighbor's, but Toren said it was at another friend's. I couldn't really smell alcohol on Toren, which scared me all the more. I wondered if he was high on something worse.

Toren muttered something else and Don asked again, "What did you drink?"

"From a cup."

"What?" He didn't know..

"Okay," Toren challenged us, "test me!"

Because we had previously tested his urine at a lab after the river party, Toren was ready to do it again. This idea seemed absurd because he could hardly sway to the bathroom. He tilted himself into the wall, and then couldn't give a specimen. Then he wobbled back to the great room and slumped onto the tile floor and began burping. I knew Toren would soon be sick, which relieved me because it now looked like the culprit was alcohol rather than other drugs.

We questioned Toren further, me in my blue bathrobe and flip-flops, Don in his tee shirt and shorts. It was the standard, 'Where were you? What were you doing? Who *were you with? Why are you doing this?' indoctrination. With little cooperation and a slur of jumbled denials, Toren swore he wasn't with anyone. But we had seen him on the street with two people. Absent was the thoughtful, gracious and cheerful kid we'd raised. I wished we had not gone to the concert. Then he began throwing up. I smelled alcohol for sure.*

Don got out the video camera and filmed Toren trying pathetically to swagger down our hallway, trying to answer my questions as I perched at our kitchen table looking extremely perturbed. He made Toren stand and asked him questions to which Toren could hardly respond. He filmed Toren retching. "Toren'll never remember this," Don told me. (I couldn't believe it. How could anyone forget a thing like this? It shows how naïve I was.)

I couldn't get through to Toren. It was as though he wasn't inside his body. He had no soul. Just spitting and syllables. He didn't seem to have any idea what he was doing.

To solve the riddle of what had happened, I called a girl with blond hair, Hillary, whom I suspected had been with Toren on the street that night. (Yes, I called her at 1:00 a.m. on a Thursday.) She claimed she had not been with him. I told her we were worried about Toren and needed to know what he had ingested. It crossed my mind that Toren could get worse, might lose consciousness. She said she'd call around to find out.

Meanwhile, Toren wanted to lie down. We were worried because he was so out-of-it. Hillary called back and said she'd talked to some people who were with Toren and that he'd had seven beers, best estimate. We were shocked. Hillary was guarded with her information, but I sensed that she wanted to help us. I knew better than to ask more.

Toren asked us to leave him alone so he could sleep. Don explained that it would be irresponsible for us to let him fall into a deep sleep because of the potential for vomiting or aspiration. (An anesthesiologist, he specializes in rendering people senseless, and he recognized when someone was in potential jeopardy. He also knew the risks of overdoses and alcohol poisoning.) So we had Toren sleep on the floor of our bedroom beside our bed and we took watchful care of him that night.

Toren woke up frequently, spitting up all over our bedroom carpet. I tried to give him a drink of water, holding up his head, but he spit into the glass. It's the only time Don and I laughed. Toren looked pathetic. As he lay there I thought about him willfully chugging down seven beers. It was disgusting to me. I felt so bad for him and wondered why he would do it. A 3.79 GPA, friends galore, nice house, summer job. Why?

The next morning, Toren did not remember a thing, did not seem to have a hangover, and wondered why he was in our bedroom. He walked calmly to his own room where we allowed him to sleep a few more hours.

When he awoke the second time later that morning, we asked Toren what he had done the night before and he said, "I went to Lakefair." (Lakefair is a summer festival in Olympia.) He had no memory of being sick, sleeping in our bedroom, or our conversations. In fact, he appeared incredulous that we would invent such a story. He only remembers waking up the next morning and being tired.

Then we showed him the video. "I never want to see that again," he told us.

After over twenty-four hours of phone calls and discussions, a story finally came through. Toren told us that he'd bought the beer at Safeway. We aren't sure that his brother didn't buy it for him, and Toren may be trying to protect him. It turns out that Toren and four other boys had partied at our house and at a tree farm near our house. Another girl, named Sara, and one of Toren's friends were not walking with Toren innocently as we had thought, but literally holding him up like a Gumby doll and helping him vomit on the way home. Had Don and I stopped by, I think *we would have noticed. It's amazing Toren made it home at all.*

Toren does remember having friends and girls over, drinking two beers, but after that, only his friends know. He's been quite forthright with us, even though there must be more to the story.

Don and I have decided not to let Toren get his drivers' license until six months after his sixteenth birthday. That will be soon enough. And that's only if we have no more incidents.

The previous admission describes how I felt at the time of Toren's virgin drunken debut: Helpless and Devastated. It's "lucky" none of us knew what we would yet go through.

We did a few things right. We went over Toren's behavior; we thought he had given us a mostly truthful story. We emphasized to him the risks in drinking so much. Don had the foresight to video Toren. But in retrospect, as we talk with Toren now, he tells us that he barely remembers seeing the tape! How can this be possible? It's because he was still too inebriated the next day to recall what he was doing. If Don and I had realized this, we would have waited to show him the video until several days later when his brain function had restored itself. The impact of our video would have been stronger. It wasn't until Toren was out of rehab nine years later that we reviewed this event with him and realized the ineffectiveness of our efforts! That's what caused me to dig out my journal and then, to my dismay, review what I *thought* had happened.

At the time of the incident, though, Don and I believed we'd made an impact and that Toren would long remember this dismal experience. While talking to him later that day, I cried and told him that it had caused me great sadness to see him abusing himself that way when I had been so careful during my pregnancies not to drink alcohol. I could not understand why he would drink so heavily. He seemed too young and too talented for such destruction. We levied consequences and hoped that Toren would respond well to them. He was a good sport, apologized, and said he was sorry. He did not make excuses for his bad behavior and followed all of our penalties, as he always did throughout the years. The start of our nightmare.

Why Toren and not other kids? As I look back, Toren navigated grade school on a narrow margin of charm. His charisma and antics could crack up any well-behaved group of kids so that they turned into uncontrollable goons. You could say teachers kept a close eye on him. Maybe that was a sign he would become addicted to alcohol, but it was never on his report card. Toren was considered the kid to talk to, the one who had all sorts of classmates calling him for advice and consolation, even though he was also considered mischievous by his teachers.

Middle school saw him beginning to smell like teen spirit, influenced by Kurt Cobain and Nirvana. He still kept up his grades, played select soccer, and talked openly to us about his life. Lots of friends came to the house, and there were girls in and out.

High school didn't seem as innocent. Toren continued to joke with our family, contribute around the house, and hold summer jobs. He did everything a parent could ask and had a great attitude. Toren was fun to be around. However, when it came to the weekends, we were always suspicious that something was going on. A sort of mischief followed Toren, always with a grin and a wink. We tried to be aware of what he was doing and with whom, as parents of early teens are, but in retrospect, I'm afraid we were often in the dark.

Some people would tell me that the reason Toren became addicted to alcohol was because we didn't have God on our side. Of course, they mean their brand of God. We didn't attend the correct church, hadn't done what good Christians would do in educating our children. I wonder if other Gods would have liked to help us? Okay, I'm calling them out. Step up to the plate, all available Gods! Whichever one will help, I'll take.

I know several religious drunks. Even some ministers who have been through rehab. (They must not have had God on their side, either.) Which God gets the credit for this? Our God-fearing U.S.A. has difficulty grappling with this disease called alcoholism even with the recovering President we have currently elected to office. We would rather ignore it or point fingers. The moral high road to addiction is a lofty one. It would be much easier to carry some sort of religious banner for deflecting criticism and the silent looks of condemnation that I anticipate from our perfect extended family, especially the devout branch. I dread telling them about Toren. Luckily, I don't have to—yet.

Toren has been at his inpatient rehab now for a week. Don and I wonder how he's doing, how he's dealing with what they are teaching him. The 12-Step Program's Higher Power would certainly be emphasized. Which Higher Power is best for the battle? We wonder how Toren will handle this part of his program since he does not embrace any particular religion. Then we receive our first letter where he talks about this very struggle:

> *My biggest problem so far is dealing with GOD. This is a 12-Step Program and God is the final source and reason for no less than every single testimony and story of recovery. There is no way around it, the foundation of it all. The initial step is admitting powerlessness over a substance and turning it over to an 'acknowledged' Higher Power as we understand it. So on Day Two, I had a session with my journal and decided to give myself a working definition of 'God' or my Higher Power so I wouldn't cringe through every prayer said the next four weeks. I decided that the combination of family, friends, nature—both perfect and imperfect—and music create a resource of power, an inspiration and a will greater than me that I could equate with God. And that will provide me the strength to do what I need to in order to get through this. This allows me to invest my energy into this program without feeling like I'm selling myself out.*

At the same time Toren is working on his spiritual orientation, a group of Tibetan monks is visiting Olympia to create a Mandala, a circular geometric pattern that represents the world in its divine form. These enlightened monks travel to various towns to promote healing and peace by constructing a beautiful design composed of colored sand. It takes over thirty hours to complete the intricate design, and when finished, they sweep the 5-foot-by-5-foot pattern away as a manifestation of *life's impermanence*, how nothing is ever the same or lasts forever. Both the creation and the destruction of the Mandala are meaningful expressions of lessons in life. Don and I check in on the monks during the week to watch them meditate and build the Mandala. We are pleased to see them because they remind us of our travels in the Spiti area of Northern India.

On Tuesday night, the monks perform traditional dances, chants and blessings in a sacred celebration. Don and I join the candlelit parade as the grains of sand are carried to Puget Sound at high tide, bright orange robes illuminated by a full moon across inky waters. Through crisp air dotted by points of flame, long brass horns plead. There the monks toss multi-colored sand into the mirrored liquid. We are given one small vial of sand to pass on to Toren, a poignant symbol for his healing and the impermanence of his disease. Don and I are hopeful that Toren will conquer this addiction. We embrace the monks' energy so that we can integrate it into our family, to honor the steps Toren is taking. During the ceremony, we hold hands as we march to the dock, determined that the symbolic act of setting the sands free will also release our son.

There is no way to tell Toren what we have done because we cannot contact him during his rehab. The small container of sand stays on top of my dresser until I can deliver it to Toren later. I will write him a letter explaining the meaning.

Each day during Toren's rehab, I send a card, an old photo, something to remind him of his family, his center. I want him to think about the different phases of his life, to reflect on how he evolved to his present situation. One day, I send him a description his paternal grandmother wrote about eating Jell-O molded in the snow banks of Nebraska in 1929, describing how thrilling it was because Jell-O was a novelty, how you could only have it in the winter when the snow would set it up. I want Toren to understand that even the simplest things can be startling and beautiful—*fresh*. The rehab facility has told us not to send food or books or magazines. Toren is supposed to be concentrating on 12-Step literature and his recovery. I wonder how making Jell-O during a snowstorm fits in, but it doesn't seem to matter.

In the past, Toren has always been diligent about tackling goals. He seems to have decided on the course of his recovery with the same absolute determination. I do not sense him faltering, even though he did not want to leave South America. But it's early; I can't believe he's only been in the program one week. To me, it seems like ten years already. It is still difficult for me to go out in public even though I have errands to do. I go to the bank but forget which account I'm accessing; I leave my car keys on top of the gas pump; I forget why I am walking into a store. When I think of my best friends, it makes me tearful because I don't want to talk of my family to them. I wish I could scream out what has happened, yet I am unable to maintain composure. I neglect to return phone calls. Certainly, I must be making too much of this. Our son's life isn't that hopeless. But to me, seeing his dreams shattered is overwhelming. I feel guilty for having participated in it.

On the same day that the packet arrives from the rehabilitation facility with the alcohol history form, Toren's therapist calls us. She says that she will be calling weekly. Gretchen assures us that Toren is very motivated, very young, and very naïve about his problem. He is doing well and will be able to call us later this week. Toren will be allowed two ten-minute calls every week. If he doesn't have visitors on Sunday, he can have an additional call that day, too. Visitors must be approved, and anyone who 'used' with him is not allowed. (Are *we* allowed? I wonder what 'using' means.)

Gretchen questions me about alcoholism in our family and our level of support for Toren. I inquire about the packet that has arrived in the mail just that day and I tell her we have attached a family alcohol history for her information. We talk about Toren's work in South America and she says no way will Toren be allowed to return. I ask her if perhaps there is room to reconsider at the end of his rehab and she says no. She explains that the counselors do not tell Toren at the beginning about the impossibility of him returning. It's because he has to come to that realization by himself. Toren needs to be the one to say that he's not capable on his own. My heart sinks when I hear this. Gretchen tells me that Toren will be released in about twenty-eight days, Monday, the 27th of October, if all goes well.

11

PARTY MY FACE OFF

We're gonna bury ourselves in cans,
Duct tape bottles to our hands,
And when there's nothing else to do
The keg's gonna make our plans.

Toren Volkmann, *Alcohology*

6 October 2003. My therapist gave me the first steps of my
treatment plan which said, "Toren lacks understanding of addiction
evidenced by his statement that he did this to himself and he
deserves it...Toren will internalize the disease process and identify
the severity of his disease."

After my original shock, amazed that she was bold enough to
say that I lacked an understanding, I tried to relax and let the
professional do her work. Through some assigned readings, I
learned a bit more about alcoholism, the role of genetic inheritance,
and how it is chronic, progressive, and potentially fatal. Basically,
plenty of time-tested evidence suggests that alcoholism and
addiction, in itself, is passed on genetically and is a disease. In
more blunt terms, it is a brain disorder that doesn't go away, only
gets worse and will kill you if not properly treated and arrested.
Maybe I should keep reading.

The process of breaking down denial doesn't happen in one
day. It took me at least another week-and-a-half of exposure and
kicking my own ass for me to be able to say, "I'm an alcoholic,"
and know what it meant. But did I really know what it meant or

believe it? It is pretty hard to know whether or not you're being honest with yourself.

A good visual way of understanding the progression of my disease was by looking at an alcohol dependency model called the Jellinek Curve. Along this curve are exhibited the symptoms one experiences with the progression of addiction. Everyone experiences it differently, but it seemed that my physical dependence and withdrawal symptoms progressed extremely rapidly.

I was told to identify all symptoms listed throughout the early, middle, and late stages of alcoholism. I related to many subtle increments that were indications: I never left a drink unfinished, whether it was mine or not. There was never an excuse that would keep me from social events we often referred to as parties, but if it was a dry event I could think of a hundred reasons I would be busy. Little things like this, that always seemed normal, appear early in the stages of alcoholism, but at that time there is no reason to examine them as a problem. For me, in fact, it didn't seem a problem. I was very typical in being able to identify with almost everything listed.

As the curve moved into the middle stage (for example the effort to control drinking but failing repeatedly), I was even more typical because I neglected to identify certain things that I couldn't relate to because 'I wasn't *that* bad.' DENIAL. Luckily, my therapist was there to point out lots of those other characteristics for me.

I was a drunk from the time I started. While it never seemed wrong in the party atmosphere, it was always my way of thinking that there was no point in drinking just one or two drinks. I always drank to get hammered. A lot of people do, but not all go down the same path, I guess. I need to remember that one or two drinks are just as pointless, or even more so now, because I won't stop. Most learned drunks will agree that one is too many and a thousand isn't enough. I get it, ha, ha.

Although I drank more than the average person in quantity and frequency, there were and are no definite telltale signs of alcoholism in the early stages. This is what was so devastating to me and is to the alcoholic. What happens is a complete deception and twisting of one's perception through time. I fell in love with the wonder drink because it made an already awesome life so damn much better. It made things so great that, even if it partially interfered with other aspects of my life, I could let them be compromised or justified in order to keep the party alive. That is what it's about, right? Being flexible and having a good time. Maybe so, but that doesn't have to entail being blind to pain, problems and potential disaster.

In hindsight, or maybe from the parents' eyes, warning signs are a bit more obvious. But to a high schooler who is just cracking his first beers and getting a taste of a new life of [fill in the blank with parents' worst nightmares], these alleged warning signs are more fittingly seen as validation, battle scars, a right-of-passage or any other youth's skewed misinterpretation. Besides, I seemed to be very good at finding myself at the wrong place at the wrong time. Whenever I was caught, it was bad luck and not my fault for doing what everyone else did, too.

At the beginning of high school in 1995, with my favorite group of friends, we were pretty open to trying anything and I certainly thought we were on the forefront of exploration. What started as simple experimentation of marijuana and drinking resulted in our new way of socializing every weekend. This was nothing abnormal and it became our way of life. Whether someone's parents were out of town, or whether we congregated at a park, in deeper wooded areas or private undeveloped areas, we'd always go out boozing or getting high. From that point, it didn't really matter what we did, whether it be in a car picking up fast food, at someone's house, or at a more formal party. We were content with our recreational use, often too wasted or stoned to really care to figure out what 'other people' did. As far as we were concerned, we *were* it, and I'm not sure I can argue. We loved getting messed up, making asses out of ourselves, and being kids. On the other side, we were all above-average athletes, reasonable students and participated normally in all the school activities—we just had more fun; it wasn't our fault.

I started out my freshman football season with high hopes. Within a week or two I felt a bit indifferent, maybe too cool or too wimpy, but either way, I quit. Unfortunately, a pattern of me not being able to complete an entire season began to surface by the

OurDrink

Crucial Phase

- ❑ Occasional relief drinking
- ❑ Constant relief drinking
- ❑ Increase in alcohol tolerance
- ❑ Onset of memory blackouts
- ❑ Surreptitious drinking
- ❑ Increasing dependence on alcohol
- ❑ Unable to discuss problem
- ❑ Decrease in ability to stop drinking
- ❑ Persistent remorse
- ❑ Promises and resolutions fail
- ❑ Loss of other interests
- ❑ Work and money troubles
- ❑ Unreasonable resentments
- ❑ Neglect of food
- ❑ Physical deterioration

Chronic Phase

- ❑ Urgency of first drinks
- ❑ Feelings of guilt
- ❑ Memory blackouts increase
- ❑ Drinking bolstered by excuses
- ❑ Grandiose and aggressive behavior
- ❑ Efforts to control fail repeatedly
- ❑ Try geographical escapes
- ❑ Family and friends avoided
- ❑ Loss of ordinary will power
- ❑ Tremors and early morning drinks
- ❑ Decrease in alcohol tolerance
- ❑ Onset of lengthy intoxication
- ❑ Moral deterioration
- ❑ Impaired thinking
- ❑ Drinking with inferiors
- ❑ Undefinable fears
- ❑ Unable to initiate action
- ❑ Obsession with drinking
- ❑ Vague spiritual desires
- ❑ All alibis exhausted
- ❑ Complete defeat admitted

**Obsessive drinking continues
in vicious cycle**

CRUCIAL PHASE

CHRONIC PHASE

86

Rehabilitation

- Honest desire for help
- Learns alcohol is an illness
- Told addiction can be arressted
- Stops taking alcohol
- Meets normal and happy
  former addicts
- Takes stock of self
- Right-thinking begins
- Spiritual needs examined
- Physical overhaul by doctor
- Onset of new hope
- Start of group therapy
- Appreciation of possiblities
  and new way of life
- Diminished fears of the
  unknown future
- Return of self-esteem
- No more desire to escape
- Adjustment to family needs
- New interests develop
- Rebirth of ideals
- Appreciation of values
- Confidence of employers
- Contentment in sobriety
- Increasing tolerance

Recovery

- Regular nourishment taken
- Realistic thinking
- Natural rest and sleep
- Family and friends
  appreciate efforts
- New circle of stable friends
- Facts faced with courage
- Increase of emotional control
- First steps toward economic
  freedom
- Care of personal appearance
- Rationalizations recognized
- Group therapy/mutual help
  continue

**Life opens up to higher levels
than ever before**

end of my sophomore year. The second, third, and fourth times I didn't finish the season had nothing to do with deciding to quit. I was kicked off. I racked up two MIPs [alcohol]—that got me kicked off the soccer teams my first two seasons. I was kicked off the football team for smoking tobacco on campus my sophomore year, and those were the times I got caught.

It would be wrong of me to leave out that in 1998, my senior year, I was also suspended from school for two weeks. After drinking, I was involved in verbally instigating a fight in the stands at a basketball game. I didn't physically participate, but the tussle got out of hand. Attempting to avoid trouble, I nearly hit the vice-principal with my car as I tried to leave the school campus. My bad. Even though I was a more-than-proud co-captain of the swim team, the faculty wasn't impressed. Therefore, I wasn't able to speak at or attend our final banquet. Guess how much of an impact that had on me? Jack shit. And Jack left town.

The problem of my repeated removal from sports teams wasn't enough for me to re-evaluate my behavior as a whole. Instead I worked on modifying my use or activity at certain times, in specific situations or seasons, to avoid getting caught or punished. I always felt terribly guilty for what I put my parents through. They had such high expectations for me. I knew that in their eyes, I was closing doors, missing out on great experiences and really just suffering from my bad decision-making. I still chose A over B again and again. And again. The sick part is, I still don't regret it. I loved sports but, ya know.

One could say that these were warning signs of alcoholism...but one could also shut the hell up. Back then, I wasn't going to listen to anybody and they could stick their expertise up their own....As it turns out, they would have had a good hypothetical point, but I wasn't ready. I was young, ready to rock, and didn't need advice. Nothing's changed. Besides, rather than chalk all that up to alcoholism or saying that my disease made me do it, I think it's pretty clear that I wasn't the best decision-maker. The argument that I'm a risk-taker and a bit impulsive may hold water to this day. Nothing's changed. But the disease was always with me and I had various times where red flags alerted the whole family that something wasn't normal in the Volkmann household.

There were two occasions, both extremely ugly, where I was 'discovered' by my parents in more than poor form. My first of such alarming incidents was an evening where my parents had gone up to Seattle for a chamber music festival. Bad move—always. About ten to twelve of us, including one of my brothers and some of his friends, started the evening off pounding ice beers. We did our thing for awhile and, still able to make decisions, we cleaned up and left before the folks got home. We headed out to a nearby tree farm to finish the job. Scene missing.

Eventually, torn-up as all hell, I guess my good buddy walked me home and dumped me off at my house, hardly able to talk. My parents met their obliterated son who was unable to say what'd happened to him. I barely enunciated to them, "I drank whatever's in the cup." That was my blacked-out attempt to rid myself of the blame. Pretty good for someone operating at a two-year-old brain level.

In the morning, I woke up confused and throbbing with a glass of water beside my bed that I didn't remember getting. I was 'invited' to watch a video by Mom and Dad. Oh, shit, it was over now. There I was dry heaving and trying to answer questions which I was incapable of understanding. I barely remember watching the video, I was still so trashed. But I know I was pretty surprised, embarrassed and felt horrible about all the shock, disappointment and concern I could see in my parents. It hurt. Damn. That wasn't part of the plan.

My brothers probably thought I must have been stupid to get that ridiculously drunk and come home like that, at fifteen-years-old. I didn't mean to. Later my mom cried to me, telling me how sad it was to see her baby destroy himself like that after all the effort, sacrifice and care put into raising me. I felt like the biggest pile of shit, but not big enough to change. That afternoon, I went to soccer practice and still smelled like alcohol. We didn't talk about it too much after the fact. I'd grow out of it, right?

Spring of my junior year in 1997, another good friend and I were dating two senior cheerleaders. Yeah, that's right, whoopee. I'll laugh with you. But this meant, of course, that we would get to double to prom, and stay out and reap the benefits of being with the older and more culturally advanced seniors. It was soccer season and our team kicked ass so I was under a super-close eye due to my two year history of breaking the shit out of what we called 'Code.' I tried to make a deal with my parents that, if I didn't drink, I could stay out all night and do what all the seniors were doing. Mom and Dad didn't agree. And I didn't see eye-to-eye with them.

So I came home at midnight, as expected, proud and sober, and declared that I'd be returning to the festivities. Because I was sober, everything was cool and I'd earned it. I woke up in the morning in a hotel with my girlfriend and still sober. No big deal. I had done what I was supposed to, in my eyes. I held up my end of the deal while everyone else got shit-faced. (I assume they did; I know that's what I would've done.) Then I marched straight over to the heaps of left-over hard alcohol from the night before (a drink that I usually didn't have a chance to 'sample') and poured myself a nice congratulatory drink. Cheers.

No more than a few hours later, I was ridiculously drunk, out of control and out of line. What I thought would be just a few harmless drinks got me beyond wasted. And fast. I was pretty much blacked-out and on my own little agenda the rest of that Sunday afternoon. Apparently I had a lot of unwanted opinions, and things were coming out of me completely uncensored and unwarranted. I refused to let anyone else drive. (The next time I got into the car, my eardrums were offended at how loud I had cranked the music up.)

That evening I woke up, or came to, after 'napping,' still in a haze and began arguing with my parents...still totally in denial that I had gotten that drunk. I was pissed because I had gloated about how responsible my conduct had been, and then I had completely eclipsed it all with this jackass maneuver. I raged, and when my mom tried to hug me, I was so disgusted, angry, and closed-off that I actually pushed her. I was completely out of character and it felt terrible. I still remember that feeling today and it was just wrong.

I'm not sure what type of punishment ensued after this outburst. I'm sure it sucked. My parents' punishments were notoriously the worst of anyone we knew. They were more severe in the amount or types of social privileges revoked as well as duration. Being grounded in the Volkmann household was never taken lightly, not subject to change or exception, and always irreversible. There was no such thing as being out on good behavior, either, for plenty of reasons. This particular time was a big deal to me and I'm sure it was damaging to my parents, maybe more so to their trust in me.

The red flags were once again up. What was wrong with me? Nothing, I thought. I chalked it up as a symptom of the good life, brushed it off, and moved on. Besides, it happened under the legal/school radar, so you're damn straight I completed the soccer season.

As our glorious high school days were coming to a close in 1998, all of us seniors had our eyes on the horizon and I made visits to several colleges for various reasons. These were my first glimpses of what college life could be like. I visited a friend of the family at a Seattle school first. Then I took a weekend in San Diego to preview the school I would head to next fall. Following that I planned to visit my brother on the East Coast to see what it was all about for him.

Being a young visitor to a college campus is a privilege, an exciting time for a high schooler. It was obvious on my visits that I was inexperienced and eager to be away. Up in Seattle, in all the excitement, I got extremely trashed and I blacked out in someone's dorm room. I turned a mellow movie night for all of them into an intoxicating show as I was transformed from innocent and well-mannered to a vomiting and needing to be babysat and just out-of-line drunk. So I heard. The next weekend in San Diego, I heard I was lucky to make it back across the border from Tijuana and woke up with gum in my hair. Whatever. So it goes.

On my visit to my brother's Eastern campus we had a great time. On our last night there, I avoided getting arrested despite my ridiculous involvement in a rather serious altercation on that campus. Upon my lucky release from the police station, I waited for the rest of the guys who were still in jail, with a half-full keg all for me and another guy. Needless to say, there was quite a homecoming party for the arrested folk upon their late return. I was gone. I woke up in my own urine, which had soaked into my luggage—I guess packed sometime before passing out on top of it. That morning, walking to the train station, I opened my eyes and saw a truck stopped and my thumb up. I must have been hitchhiking. I made it to the station where I passed out again.

My brothers found me and got us to Manhattan where we were headed. We had a nice tour through Harlem with my pants ripped all the way down one urine-soaked inseam. I was pretty well off considering I didn't go to jail, where I belonged the night before. If my parents had found out what really went on, they might have seriously reconsidered allowing me to go to college in San Diego.

Were all these classy visits to other campuses rehearsals for my behavioral outbursts during my college freshman year? Hell no. I was just getting my green feet wet and still learning the ropes. There was no problem. I was still in high school. Relax. (And don't think, "Gee, man, it sure is surprising that no one ever pulled you aside and said, 'You know, I think some of these things are pretty scary. Maybe you have a problem and should think about getting help.'")

No, it's not surprising *that* never happened, because most of these things went under the radar of any counselor, authority, and more importantly, the parents. You think I went home and when asked, "Hey, Toren, how was your night last night?" that I responded, "Oh, it was great. I drank a 40 oz under 5 minutes; we made a double-funnel beer bong; we outran the cops; and later, I blacked out and woke up in a strange bathroom with my pants on inside out. How was yours?" Never. There was always a normal activity or at least a smoothed-over version of what we were up to, the imaginary side of the coin of my perfect teenager life. There was no friend of mine who would suggest to another that anyone had a problem because it was all too early and too fun. What could possibly go wrong in our worlds?

The law. Throughout college I had numerous near arrests and encounters with police. Although it was socially implicit and acceptable to drink much earlier, ironically, as it became legal to drink, we thought all our troubles would go away. Damn it. There were still rules of conduct and order to be broken, and it was increasingly possible for me, in the college atmosphere, to find these situations.

The focus was driving while intoxicated, or public drunkenness.

I basically didn't drink and drive most of the time because I always planned on drinking and the odds of getting caught were just too high. As if I'd actually do something that endangered people. Not that I never drove drunk, but I usually just compromised by getting drunk rather than trying to get other places or trying to be everywhere all the time. My complacency was a good decision. Yaaay.

So I avoided that, but man could I get drunk in public. After my final underage charge for possession of alcohol my sophomore year in college at age twenty, I upgraded and quickly found myself in trouble with public intoxication charges. To spare details, in 1999, I found myself in the same Santa Barbara County drunk tank with my jailwich, apple, and milk, two different times—both for stupid reasons, but always intoxicated. My final visit to a drunk tank was in San Francisco, a mere five months before entering the Peace Corps. It seemed the cops were almost as out of line as I was. (My parents knew nothing about it.) Luckily the charges were dropped. I was pretty good and skunked though, you have to give them that much.

12

A Few Missed Parties

EXAMINING TOREN THROUGH THE UNDERSIDE OF A DRAINED BEER GLASS distorts his adolescence; there's more to him than a trash can full of empties. I consider his artwork, his trophies and ribbons, his acts of largesse and compassion, his ability to communicate and put people at ease—all the things kids amass in American culture to show their aptitude and expertise. But standing in the way is a viscosity which alters and devastates the outcome. It erects a barrier between what we parents learn about our son, and ultimately what we do about it. What drains through, after all, is our son's continual pursuit of pleasure in bottled form.

During his high school years, Don and I found beer hidden in the bushes and wine coolers stowed in the car trunk. A few times we smelled alcohol on Toren's breath. His accomplishments became diluted over time by these findings, even though we tried to emphasize athletics, academics, and Toren's positive role within our family. It's true that Toren was a pleasure to have at home. He was willing to talk about his goals and remained positive in listening to our suggestions. We talked about his flirtation with alcohol and ensuing bad decisions, and he agreed they weren't helping him. He always pointed out how he was improving his life, how he was mostly achieving what he wanted. We gave ourselves hope by stressing Toren's successful activities and his loving persona.

Toren snuck around to a certain degree but, by his junior year, he grew bolder about what he wanted. An example of Toren's classic 'Eyes-Open Rebellion' occurred when we insisted that he come in by midnight on prom night his junior year. First, he argued to stay out all night with his girlfriend (who was a senior, a cheerleader, an honors student). When we said absolutely not, Toren came home as we requested. He proved to us he had not been drinking and told us about the dinner and dance. But then he went right back out. Later the next day, he finally returned home in the afternoon. Toren had calmly warned us that he was going to stay out all night no matter what, and said that he would pay the penalty for doing so. He assured us that we could ground him for a year, he didn't care; it would be worth it. We guessed that he spent the night at a hotel in town partying with friends (while we spent a sleepless night worrying). And we had every right to worry, because the next day it appeared he had driven home after consuming a huge quantity of vodka. In broad daylight, Toren sauntered into the house wearing tuxedo pants, his shirt open, and promptly fell asleep in an alcoholic stupor. It was difficult to rouse him from his sweaty sleep. I remember it vividly and I recall thinking how powerless I felt.

Don and I had had a long discussion. Then we tried to talk with Toren about being responsible for his own decisions, closing doors to opportunity by unthinking behaviors, the costs of legal fees for underage drinking, and maintaining control of his life. Toren said he knew what he was doing, that he appreciated our concern and understood that we were trying to do our jobs as parents. He said whatever penalty we imposed, he would do. His attitude was not as cooperative as usual. In fact, this time he was hostile. I can no longer remember exactly the consequences we levied. Usually we took away driving privileges, phone time, or assigned books to read or jobs to do, and restructured his social time with friends. It always calmed things down. Toren had to walk to school the remainder of that spring, but he assured us it was good exercise and that he deserved it for staying out all night. We weren't sure how often he was drinking, but the few times we had previously managed to catch him, he had seemed extremely intoxicated. We worried about this. Should we have shipped him off to rehab then? He was starting on the varsity soccer team and pulling good grades. Don and I continued our discussion with Toren, thinking somehow we would get through to him. It kept us on edge.

In retrospect, I'd say yes, it had been time for an intervention or rehab program for Toren. But remember that he was still lying to us about the extent of his drinking. We still thought that the times we caught him were the majority of his alcohol experiences. Ultimately, I don't know whether a rehab program during high school would have been successful without Toren's willingness. He did not seem ready to admit that alcohol was holding him back. His life was a success from his point of view, and he didn't hesitate to tell us so.

One night about this same era, I had a chamber music gig away from the house. Don was working at the hospital. I returned home after the job sooner than Toren—and about thirty of his friends—expected. They had taken over the house and were listening to music, sitting around our kitchen and great room, talking and drinking. I was able to stand for some time in our unlit entryway where I'd entered undetected and listen to their banter. Hearing several of Toren's friends, I knew exactly who was in attendance. Eventually, I was spotted there holding onto my viola, still in my coat. The guilty drinking kids began pouring out the back door, some through the garage, some sailing right past me. I heard them trying to start their cars; a bottle broke in the street, some guys yelled to each other. It was pandemonium for a few minutes. When the confusion cleared, a corps of kids remained at the kitchen table. They greeted me somewhat sheepishly and I sat down with them. I noticed all of them were drinking only soft drinks. Toren joined us uneasily. In fact, he looked as though a guillotine might at any moment fall across his neck.

We talked about high school, their classes, plans for college, what they were doing at our house ("Partying. Thank you, Mrs. Volkmann."). The remaining kids were in no rush to leave because they'd been drinking non-alcoholic beverages. I knew and liked them (in fact I even liked the kids who'd fled without saying good-bye). Finally, after everyone had left, Toren began pacing around the house, knowing we needed to work things out. He and I talked about the growing breach of trust, the responsibility of holding such events unchaperoned at our home, the deep disappointment I felt. We agreed to some terms and penalties much the same as writing up a no-fault divorce with two like-minded parties. It seemed this phase of the war was already over. We held onto a détente where we elected not to talk anymore about what had happened. Each time we were repeating the same phrases to one another. It was too depressing for me, and Toren sensed I was at the end of my ability to deal with it. I don't think we even told Toren's dad. Neither of us could bear to hurt him again.

Toren shaped up, after that, for some time. At least, we weren't aware of anything going on. He talked to us often about his determination not to party, how he was standing up to social pressure. We made it through summer to the fall of his senior year of high school, then we made it on through football season. But, during the winter swim season, it ended. Toren appeared intoxicated at a basketball game (as a spectator), verbally harassed opposing fans, and practically ran over a vice-principal in the parking lot. For this, Toren was suspended from high school for ten days. At that same time, Toren had been enrolled in a serious Shakespeare class. He wanted to see a performance of *The Twelfth Night* in Tacoma with his class, but this was denied because of his suspension, as well as being forbidden to attend the Swim Team Banquet (he was co-captain of the swim team). Toren had worked hard in swimming and adored Shakespeare, so he was extremely disappointed. This punishment truly was a low point for Toren, we thought. We were sure he must have hit bottom and that a real turn-around would take place.

Toren missed a few parties as a result of his latest misstep. He spent a lot of time with his parents and family during his suspension and, again, lost driving and phone privileges. It gave us all time to think. We encouraged him to make it through soccer season, his final high school sport, without an incident. He was about to graduate from high school. It was time for him to apply for a summer job and to focus on college. Toren assured us his wild ways were diminishing, since he'd already 'done it all' in high school. He talked with us about drinking and partying, and said he was planning on making it through graduation without any alcohol. I don't know if he did or not. But he stayed out of trouble, at least. I looked forward to sleeping better at night.

Each time he was kicked off a team, not only did Toren miss the end-of-the season celebration, but so did we, his parents. Throughout our kids' youth, Don and I attempted to support them in their interests. With the public schools, this usually meant coordinating booster club activities or participating on fundraising committees. We both contributed during soccer, football, and swim team seasons, which took hours of our time. It was a method of showing our boys that we valued their activities, that we cared. Don acted as president of the soccer parent boosters for six seasons straight and volunteered as the football on-field doc for eight years. I worked as president of the high school Parent Connection, a group committed to bettering communications between high school and home. It was not only disappointing, but embarrassing to attend these events without our son (as we were obligated to do sometimes) or not go and know that people would be second guessing about why we were suddenly absent.

Just today, I heard experts talking on the radio about drugs and alcohol and high school kids, about how families with addicts are usually families where no one cares what the kids are doing. 'They' said that, in high school, parents all but disappear; that parents stop attending conferences or events for their kids. And I've heard the opposite as well, that parents don't let their kids work things out on their own. In this case 'they' say that many parents are over-involved, too pushy, too in-your-face with their kids, always trying to rescue their darlings or cover up for them. I wish I could find them, those 'they' people, to see what 'they' say about the parties we missed on behalf of our son and the parties he missed when we could catch him. What really goes through my mind is that sometimes experts have no idea what families are attempting to accomplish with their kids and, no matter what is done, sometimes it's not enough nor does it solve the problem.

A portion of Toren's first letter from rehab talks about his early drinking:

I subscribe that there is cognitive distortion, a genetic

disposition, and other things that may be influencing how
rapidly I've experienced certain aspects (more physical than
anything) in this scary progression. Not to mention, I've
been a BINGE drinker from the start, more or less. Some
other church-going, social-drinkers with my makeup may
not have been affected for years but, for me, I think it's been
a highly reactive combo. I have very little emotional damage
or problems and few ruined relationships or law violations
compared to the other people here at rehab. I have nothing
to be bitching about and everything to live for and that is
WHY I am here NOW. This doesn't make it easy, but it is
nice not to be thinking about a fuming wife, abandoned
kids, pending charges or a vehicular homicide, or whatever
you-name-it symptom of this affliction. I'm trying to keep
an open mind and listen—and ignore thoughts about South
America. But sometimes I wonder what did I do? And why
or how it all happened so fast?

I see that Toren's pondering some of the same things as I. Like
why did it happen in the first place? I look back and remember time
after time when I attempted to tell myself *this* would be the last
time. The *last* time. No—THIS will be the last time…this time…. I
leaf through slips of paper in the 'Toren' file, flitting from episode
to episode. Why did I save those scraps of evidence if I was trying to
forget? I find several letters he wrote to the high school
administration about his suspension, where he apologizes sincerely
and requests the chance to attend the Shakespeare production, where
he talks about all the thinking he has done, the prioritizing. Is this
not the doctrine of an alcoholic: sincere remorse then on to another
foray? I wonder how I could have been so gullible. Again. And again.

Now, as a result of my preoccupation with this debacle, I miss
a party. I say no to the trumpet section when they invite me out for
a beer (really fun guys). I *could* go along and drink Perrier; I know
that. But somehow, my heart's not in it. I don't feel like talking to
anyone, especially people who will ask about my family members. I
also say no to friends calling to invite us to dinner, no to lunch on

someone's boat, no to a glass of wine after work on Friday. The perfect bubble has burst. I stay home to figure out why I didn't see my son clearly in those early days. Didn't stop him. Couldn't have helped him. (Miss a few more good parties.)

13

Beer Bong U

Well, show me the way
To the next whiskey bar
Oh, don't ask why
Oh, don't ask why

Show me the way
To the next whiskey bar
Oh, don't ask why
Oh, don't ask why

For if we don't find
The next whiskey bar
I tell you we must die
I tell you we must die
I tell you, I tell you
I tell you we must die

—The Doors, *Alabama Song - Whiskey Bar* [31]

He asked me how to wash a pillow. One of our sons called me in September of his freshman year after a rugby hazing. It didn't take much probing to discover that he had trashed his pillow being sick when the rugby club team had initiated all the freshmen.

"I told them I don't drink much, but that I'd try. But it wasn't enough for them," our son lamented.

Upperclassmen had tied one-gallon trash bags around the necks of the freshmen and commanded them to drink a beer for every year of their lives—that would be eighteen or nineteen sixteen-ounce beers. The freshmen began puking into the bags at the same time they were required to finish their quotas. Eventually, our son said, he dumped most of the drinks down his chin. He was so ill an upperclassman had to drive him back to his dorm. There he stayed in bed for two days. Now his bedding was filthy. His newly-assigned college roommate had tried to help him, but he didn't know our son well and did not realize his desperate state. He left him in the dorm room for two days of misery.

A scholarship student, our son took his studies seriously and did not relish missing classes. When I hung up the phone, it hit me how he'd changed. His voice, once so enthusiastic, sounded weak and confused. I tried to be calm when I told him how to launder the pillow, mattress pad, and the sheets. I didn't want to sound like an over-protective, crazed mother. But it broke my heart because I remembered how excitedly he had talked to his father and me about selecting a club sport, the fun of rugby practices, how he was doing on the team, the thrill of meeting guys from all over the U.S. He was a strong athlete and I knew his desire to fit in and be accepted. I saw his quandary at "getting through the initiation" so that he could survive and continue to play. Not only did it cause me sadness, but it infuriated me.

Alcohol poisoning had not been listed as a prerequisite in the college catalogue of this expensive, private university. I wanted to call the administration to tell them so. Here we were paying private tuition (not to mention buying new bedding at Linens and Things) and our son calls home telling us of team-enforced alcohol abuse. But isn't this a longstanding tradition in American higher education? Complacent parents pay money to enroll their outstanding offspring in this cycle of abuse and seeding of addiction.

Our son agreed with me that the hazing was dangerous for neophyte drinkers, that indeed he had been seriously affected. But he said if word got back that his mother had complained, he wouldn't be safe on campus. The rugby players had told him he'd get used to the drinking, that everyone'd had to go through it. After that, our son played two more games, then quit the team. At the next after-game celebration, he had not been forced to drink, but felt extremely uncomfortable. It just wasn't worth it. He later transferred to a different university. It wasn't that he didn't drink alcohol during his freshman year; the problem was being forced to drink more than he knew was safe.

According to Wechsler and Wuethrich in *Dying to Drink*, even mild hangovers are a threat to a student's academic standing.[32] Approximately 159,000 first-year college students drop out of school for alcohol- or drug-related reasons.[33] No wonder, because a hangover is unpleasant and few students care to go to class feeling under the weather. A hangover is the result of alcohol withdrawal after prolonged or heavy drinking. The symptoms, including muscle pain, headache, fatigue, nausea, jittery hands and slight anxiety, are caused by a chemical imbalance of the nerves surrounding the lining of the brain, the digestive system, and blood vessels. These effects usually begin from six to forty-eight hours after the final drink. A more severe type of withdrawal is called delirium tremens or 'DTs'. Featuring hallucinations, vivid confusion, and severe nervous system hyperactivity, DTs usually begin more than forty-eight hours after the last drink.

The swilling of alcohol on college campuses is being examined in several studies. One fact uncovered is that *underage students* (as was our rugby-playing son*) drink 48 percent of all alcohol consumed on college campuses*. This includes schools with graduate populations and older students. During fall alcohol promotions, alcohol prices are low, as cheap as twenty-five cents per beer. The drinking lifestyle is a well-advertised and low-budget form of entertainment on college campuses according to Henry Wechsler, Ph.D., Principal Investigator of the College Alcohol Study. "Our study confirms that the lower the prices and the more extensive the specials, the more heavy the drinking. What this means for programs to protect college students from destructive drinking and its consequences, is clear: they have an uphill battle."[34]

Getting to the next whiskey bar is not such a worry anymore because the alcohol outlet density—bars and liquor stores—within two miles of most campuses, is increasing.

The Harvard School of Public Health College Alcohol Study confirmed strong correlations between the saturation of alcohol outlets and risky drinking behavior among college students. Researchers actually calculated neighborhood alcohol outlet density and compared drinking-related problems to alcohol accessibility. [35] Heavy drinking at this age is associated with various levels of collegiate life—the Greeks, independent dorms and apartment commuters, as well as many college clubs and sports.

"Most college presidents are afraid to take on the problem of alcohol abuse on their campus. They think it will hurt enrollment and offend alumni who have fond memories of the haze of alcohol," states Robert Carothers, president of the University of Rhode Island. He goes on to say, "I tell them that I found just the opposite. I have very strong support in terms of enrollment patterns, support from parents and from 95 percent of the alumni. Taking a principled and intelligent stand on these issues brings good things to the president."[36]

Not only is binge drinking a phenomenon in America, other governments are researching the problem as well. Western European countries are experiencing the effects of drinking adolescents. The fact that other nations are investigating chronic heavy drinking [37] signifies international concern about the problem. Because half of the world's people are under the age of twenty-five, this is a far-reaching dilemma.[38] BBC's Margaret Gilmore reports that "there is an increasing culture of intoxication." Around 4 percent of England's medical admissions are alcohol related, and the figure rises to 70 percent between midnight and 5 a.m. British researchers are finding that the binge-drinking period that was once confined to the late teens now often runs from age sixteen to twenty-four. English ministers plan to publish strategies in 2004 tackling binge drinking and other alcohol-related problems. Lord Adebowale, chief executive of the charity, *Turning Point,* told BBC, "We are talking about families dissolving in a sea of alcohol." The chief executive of the British Beer and Pub Association, Rob Hayward, stated, "We also need to get to the root causes of what motivates a significant number of people who think it is acceptable to go out on a Friday or Saturday night, drink to excess and indulge in anti-social behaviour."[39]

Europe and the U.S. are not alone in agonizing about binge drinking. A ten-year study of 2000 teenagers in Australia found that one in twelve teens developed symptoms of alcohol dependence during the ten-year period. Professor George Patton, director of Australia's Centre for Adolescent Health, stated, "We don't have much experience (with young alcohol dependents). Nobody really knows what happens to somebody who is alcohol-dependent at the age of twenty-five."[40]

After Toren's high school experiences with alcohol, we worried he might go crazy with it in college. However, when we visited him in his first year, he seemed to be adjusting well. He did appear moderately stressed about his studies, particularly about an upper level Shakespeare class he had talked his way into. He loved the class but worried obsessively about achieving satisfactory understanding of the material and his grade. We had seen his brothers struggle in their adjustments to college during previous years and figured Toren would also learn to manage. His grades came through at a high level, even the Dean's List, and we assumed he had found his niche.

But late in the spring, Toren confessed to us that he wasn't living in the same dorm anymore because there had been an 'incident.' He'd been kicked out and was relocated. According to Toren, the incident had involved a bunch of guys on his floor drinking and being disrespectful. It was hard to dig out the whole story. But Toren said he'd found a roommate for his sophomore year and planned to live in some apartments close to campus. We did not like this, but it wasn't the first time we'd disapproved of our sons' living choices while in college. You could say that, after multiple discussions with our first two sons, we were somewhat battered down by this time. Once again, we crossed our fingers and talked and talked with Toren about his choices.

As exhibited already by Toren and his freshman dorm mates, *one-third of college students have alcohol disorders and 6 percent meet clinical criteria for dependency.*[41] Studies stress that students who drink heavily are at high risk for mental disorders and these same studies maintain that prevention programs are in need at colleges. I wonder how alcohol prevention programs would be able to attract kids such as our son and the guys on his floor? I wonder what could be done to influence a change in their drinking patterns? We parents were not notified (because that's the policy) even though *we* are the people who pay his tuition. When the infraction occurred, our son was legally under drinking age. So, in the perfectly counterbalanced family's college history, one son passes up a rugby team because of alcohol peer pressure and another epitomizes the need for programs to manage campus drinking.

Lots of students are able to survive college partying and move on without chronic damage. A campus is, after all, a setting of higher education. It is not the institution's responsibility to care for the youth we send them, to hold their hands, to predict which of them will become addicts and which of them will graduate *cum laude*. There has been an administrative movement away from cocooning college students within the protective arms of parents. Whereas colleges used to practice *parens patriea*, a type of surrogate parenthood where administration attempted to guide and nurture students, current policy has shifted away from that role and now diminishes the hovering campus guardian. It allows students to face consequences of behavior on their own. Therefore, colleges do not notify parents of students' wrongdoings. With a wink and a nod, students do what they will, functioning in the limbo of their pseudo adult/adolescent existence. After all, they're over eighteen. They can legally vote. It's time to grow up. Universities are not probation officers or babysitters. The 80 percent of students who can drink successfully will thrive. But the 20 percent who cannot will cause problems. Unfortunately, these problems become not only a campus problem, but a family problem, and thereafter society's problem. The university system is not "obligated" to take care of these people. Perhaps there could be more available tools for them when they flounder. (But even when programs or interventions are created, it is difficult to ensure that chronic abusers will seek out or utilize the services.)

A table of College Student Drinking Facts is published in *Dying to Drink* [42]:

✓ 73 percent of fraternity and 57 percent of sorority members are binge drinkers.

✓ 58 percent of male athletes and 47 percent of female athletes are binge drinkers.

✓ Frequent binge drinkers constitute less than one-quarter of all students (23 percent) but consume three-quarters (72 percent) of all the alcohol college students drink.

✓ A ring of bars and liquor stores surrounds most colleges. At one college one hundred eighty-five outlets were located within two miles of campus.

When our sons were in college, we chose not to bring them home for Thanksgiving holidays because the vacation period was short and the distance great. Because of this, they united with new and former friends, congregating in such cities as Boston, New York, Santa Barbara, and San Diego to prepare their own feast. If you removed the alcohol, the gatherings could have entertained Grandma in style. The boys usually called me while struggling through preparation of gravy or turkey and stuffing. Something always needed adjusting. But as the years ensued, I grew to dread the holiday because I knew they were drinking too much alcohol. They had shown me photos and told stories and it scared me. I found out that on one of the 'turkey holidays,' Toren was arrested for public drunkenness at 10 a.m. He called home the following week to ask us what to do about legal procedures. We told him to find a lawyer and pay for it himself. So he did. Being 2000 miles away, I had to let go. When there's a story in the newspaper, it's always the mother talking about how sweet and docile her child is, how he could never have done such a deed. I slept less well and became a worrying mother, even though I gave the appearance of leaving my son's destiny in his own hands.

We always felt that Toren should be responsible for his own actions. Just as binge drinkers should be responsible for the problems they create. Is there anyone else to blame?

One could blame alcohol promoters for providing cheap drinks which causes kids to come back for more.

Or blame the campuses and communities for not enforcing minimum-drinking-age laws.

Or blame parents for not monitoring their students' behavior or not finding out how tuition funds are being utilized.

Or even blame college presidents and administrators for turning a blind eye to sports initiations, sorority/fraternity functions and campus alcohol-inspired infractions.

The blame can be spread in many directions. Blaming someone does not get to the bottom of what is causing the problem. It is just a way to pass off ownership of a situation to which we have all contributed.

Toren pressured us to allow him to study in the Semester at Sea Program his junior year. This paralleled his interests in global studies, psychology, and world service. Considering Toren's history of high school and college alcohol problems (and that's counting only the ones we knew about), people would wonder why we would pay for this. It turns out the cost was almost comparable to college tuition. His grades were still good. We had several discussions with him. After he researched the program, applied, and convinced us that he would not fulfill the reputation some students had for calling the program 'Party at Sea' or 'Mattress at Sea,' and after he worked all summer to earn a portion of his expenses, and diligently filled out the paperwork and visa applications on his own, we said okay. It seemed safer to have Toren anchored in the middle of an ocean than frequenting the Seven-Eleven on the corner of campus. Another part of the deal was: no alcohol-related trouble during the summer prior to his study abroad.

Semester at Sea drifted by without a hitch. Toren was not shipped home early nor did he get thrown into a foreign prison. His drinking may have been less, away from his usual collegiate haunts and buddies. Aboard ship, the staff monitored each student's bar tab, closed the bars at set hours, and stressed a no-tolerance policy for drugs and alcohol in the cabins. Students were not allowed to bring alcohol aboard and were educated about proper conduct as international guests. Toren had previously traveled with our family to third world destinations and embraced our philosophy not to represent the stereotypical ugly American strangled by camera, Nikes, and money belt. This doctrine, along with astute guidance by shipboard professors and staff, seemed to outweigh Toren's penchant for alcohol mischief. He called from India and told me, "We love you." I was alarmed and asked, "WE?" "Yes, Mom, it's true. We. The world. We love you."

Moving through various college scenarios with each of our boys provided scores of experiences I could not have anticipated. The upshot is that *I finally* graduated from Beer Bong U, right along with them! Our sons ultimately gave me a private tasting of college life I will never forget. It happened when Don and I visited one of Toren's brothers at a university where he was a senior. We met his friends and they threw a party at their rented house to welcome us. However, I discovered that the true guest of honor was: Triceptatrough—the beer bong dinosaur. I had told my son to get it out of our house and he did; he took it back to college with him. There it was, hanging on the back patio in all its glory and splendor, fully operational. Let me describe this demon: the Triceptatrough was constructed of a series of mad-scientist looking funnels hooked to plastic tubes with valves which looked like they could open pipelines to an Olympic-sized swimming pool. It was activated by a main valve which flooded the apparatus with a beverage (often beer) free of air or obstruction. Bongers took their places in a line underneath individual faucets.

By now, I'd become somewhat glazed. Perhaps you could say I'd lost my perspective. I knew our son had done well in school; I'd had commensurate experience locating and discarding any number of contraband funnels; and I realized that most of the kids attending this party were age-appropriate. We had talked with every person attending the bash, and finally met all the friends described by our son for the past several years. They were delightful kids with varied talents and interests.

As the party mellowed, my husband and I watched four or five students line up under the multi-funneled contraption, then open their mouths for a round of beer to pour forth. No one appeared intoxicated except for one dude who had arrived already in that state. The kids asked if we wouldn't like to try it. Suddenly, as half-witted as it seems, Don and I said okay. After all my lectures…after the infamous green Binge Drinking Chart…after expelling the dinosaur from our home…here I was queuing up like a hardened bonger! I viewed it as an experiment, I told myself. For several years I'd been hearing about this Triceptatrough, now I would try it. The dosed quantity looked to be about the amount of one can of beer. I thought I could do it and hoped I wouldn't gag. I was nervous. When the beer burst through, I found it fast and unobtrusive. It just went down. I stepped back and it was over. I didn't feel bad. I felt like the same person.

No wonder. No wonder they do it.

The party dwindled down and my husband and I went back to our hotel. We talked about how easy it was to bong. How frightening. And we felt guilty that we had tried beer bonging, as though we were endorsing it in front of our son's friends. I guess we were. But my feelings still haven't changed. I look at binging as a dangerously seductive activity with no point. I still resent the beer bong dinosaur.

I continue to look at alcohol and its effects on our family throughout our three boys' college experiences. A creeping paranoia sets in. By now, we are unknowingly raising one alcoholic and two undiagnosed sons who admit they've done more than their share of binging. Slowly, I become worn down. Now I'm reading in the Sunday paper that I should drink a glass of red wine each day for better health. I wonder how that news will influence my sons. Is it possible to put red wine in a funnel?

I mention to my husband that beer bonging could be similar to that glass of wine at night, maybe something good for me and I don't know it. He points out that there has been much research showing that the alcohol industry is deceptive, that innumerable reports are unchallenged by media and science. The data is often misleading, unsubstantiated.

June Russell has done extensive research on the media and alcohol and suggests that original studies should be read to check out the accuracy. *Many articles about the benefits of alcohol are funded by the alcohol industry.* Press releases often omit dangers, especially when dealing with *doses* of alcohol, which are frequently harmful when increased by a single drink. There are more than four hundred substances in alcoholic beverages beside ethanol, some linked to cancer, and the alcohol industry is not required to disclose them, nor to alert the public of risks.[43] Our experience beer bonging with college students only further reinforces uneasy feelings about the seductive glamour of peer influence and blatant media distortion. My husband and I, perfect examples, succumbed to the bong and became more wary with each swallow.

The college binge drinking problem is receiving proactive attention. *Alcohol-related problems are a leading cause of morbidity in college students* and student health services are beginning to provide screening and assessment for alcohol use. The goal of such programs is to reduce alcohol-related harm. This can directly benefit students' health by reducing the estimated fourteen hundred deaths and 500,000 serious alcohol-related injuries each year.[44] In Wechsler and Wuethrich's book, *Dying to Drink*, concrete suggestions are given to families, communities and campuses for dealing with binge drinking.

One university-based urgent care worker I interviewed reported that he treated an average of twenty students per day for alcohol-related injuries. He also commented that college STD, rape, and pregnancy statistics inflate as students consume alcohol.[45] According to the College Alcohol Study, roughly one in twenty (4.7 percent) women reported being raped; nearly three-quarters (72 percent) of the victims experienced rape while intoxicated.[46] Women who attend notorious party colleges or join sororities face the highest risk. Under mounting evidence of damage by alcohol use, universities are now becoming aware of remedies for chronic heavy drinking and binge drinking.

Some colleges are getting down to business about alcohol consumption on campus. Intervention programs, even brief ones where a student is contacted three to five times, have been initiated at a number of universities to head off alcohol problems. Students can actually be screened for alcohol use disorders. There are consumption questions and staff to deal with the results in a non-punitive environment. Selected campuses have mounted specific campaigns to curb excessive student drinking. These efforts, called 'social-norms marketing,' have shown mixed success according to research published in September 2003.[47] Some students appear skeptical about alcohol education programs according to this study, and seem to align more closely to drinking behaviors of their immediate social group rather than to the overall student population at a given school. The conclusion is that students will drink no matter what. Because this research is fresh, and because it has been criticized as narrow in statistical sampling, it is not clear what would or could be effective to satisfactorily modify drinking on the college campus.[48] It even appears that such campaigns may have had the side effect of increasing alcohol consumption among two groups of light-to-moderate drinkers. Students may have increased their alcohol consumption toward "acceptable" levels.

Because alcohol doesn't have the negative stigma of tobacco, and the product is legal, it is justified and glamorous to both males to females. There's research out there about problems with alcohol, but the public hasn't synthesized it to the home drinking labs or the student housing micro bars. Obviously the college rugby team thinks it's a manhood-enhancer, and dorm buddies bond in a lather of suds. Fraternities and sororities commonly embrace drinking and underage consumption of alcohol as status quo, often as an alluring accessory for membership and initiation. Sports teams look the other way.

And parents are blind. Maybe that's because we're busy sipping wine as we bid at prestigious arts fundraisers, or we're knocking back a few tall cold ones at our alumni tailgate parties, or maybe we're out to a two-martini dinner with intimate friends while our successful kids are tucked away on campus where fun can't be categorized as dangerous. Or progressive. Or addictive.

Mid-junior year of college, Toren had his wisdom teeth extracted and survived an extensive shoulder surgery during Christmas vacation. After the surgery, I doled out pain killers to him whenever I thought he needed one. Toren acted insulted but, by this time, I was wary. Even with these medications, he seemed in a lot of pain.

Then, one day I found the stash; he hadn't taken them and was stockpiling them. I asked him why, and he said, "To sell." I became nervous once again. When I further questioned Toren, he told me he could get five dollars for each capsule. He had been willing to endure a fair amount of agony to hoard away those meds. I wondered what kind of son we had raised. I fretted.

He would be graduating from college soon. Toren took a full class load as well a preparation course for the GREs where he memorized hundreds of vocabulary words. He claimed he wanted to get the GREs out of the way so that he could use the results for grad school applications and called me frequently to chat about his psychology internship at a local children's hospital, his prep course, and his final work in school. Toren talked about applying to the Peace Corps. He could go away and be successful, escape his drinking buddies. I began counting the minutes to graduation.

Toren disappeared during spring vacations and I wrung my hands wondering what he was doing. While finishing up his junior and senior years, he racked up several physical feats such as falling into poison oak (requiring steroids for treatment) and cutting his foot on a camping trip in Mexico and thereby contracting cellulitis. During college, there were times when we wouldn't hear from him for days. I thought it was normal, because back when I went to college, I would go weeks without calling home; it was too expensive to make long distance calls. Now, I realize that a lot of parents stay in touch at least weekly, if not daily. We worried about Toren, but we wanted to give him a chance to make decisions for himself. He was succeeding as he traveled around the world on a ship, spent spring breaks and Thanksgivings with his brothers and friends, worked through his own problems, because his parents thought he should begin to learn his own way.

To the next whiskey bar.

"We ought to give him some space," we said.

Space to die. To kill himself.

Oh, don't ask why.

14

IN DESCENT

Before I entered the Peace Corps, I was clearly aware that I had a problem. I just didn't understand it.

Over my last year of college, I began to notice many new physical symptoms occurring. It made me wonder if other people were feeling the same way I did after a long weekend. Those post-drinking withdrawal symptoms (once as simple as mere sleeplessness) had slowly escalated, leaving me devastated and in pretty bad shape for the better part of my senior year. I was, in actuality, a full-blown alcoholic by college graduation, but my mindset told me that I could just party through it until I 'made it' to the Peace Corps, not really wanting to investigate the depth or reality of the problem. Much of me denied the possibility of alcoholism or that it was really an authentic problem.

Being drunk for five months straight after graduating (throughout that summer of 2002 in Seattle and on into the fall when I lived in Las Vegas) was a *choice* I made and was my way of getting the 'problem' out of my system. But, all my choices were under-the-influence in one way or another and I was really just quieting any voices inside that were starting to slowly recognize that things were not right.

Throughout my two months spent studying Spanish in Mexico, I got a feel for sobriety. There, I realized that my drinking was a self-exacerbating process and that I was better off avoiding it.

I had no alcohol in my system when I first met all my fellow Peace Corps volunteers and I intended to keep it that way. We spent a few nights together in Miami before leaving for South America and I stuck to myself, trying to lay low and avoid the inevitable socializing (which to me meant alcohol.) I went out with some girls that last night in Miami and had drinks at a club. I didn't drink much and woke up pretty normal, but my body knew what had happened. I can't tell lies to the physiological shit in my brain, stuff that *I* don't even understand. I can only kid myself—pretty effectively, too.

The next day, after some internal resistance, I had a case of the 'fukits' and had about four beers with some other new faces. Damn it, dude—why did I do that? I knew exactly why I couldn't sleep and had a fever on the plane ride down. Jackass, I thought, same result.

Upon arrival in my country of service, I would be given the opportunity to wipe the slate clean and, with this, began a trial and error period. I thought I could learn to drink around what needed to be controlled and go on with life like nothing was wrong. During my time in rehab, I have been able to look back at how it all slowly unraveled, and my therapist was there to call me out when I started bullshitting or minimizing the problems that were occurring. It was pretty easy to see what had happened.

Throughout training, I tried to be low profile and act like I was just a normal drinker. It was such a big deal to me *inside* anytime alcohol was around, I became careful, cautious and edgy. I would have no problems socializing if I could just get away from that bottled demon. I hated it already. But it didn't take long for me to get to know the other folks and realize that they were a really fun group. It also didn't take long for me to reason that it wouldn't matter if I just got past the uneasiness of the first drinks, the silencing of my internal resistance, and I could just have fun like I always did...on alcohol. Once I picked up, it followed that I would almost always drink until the last people were at the bar. And I *was* moderating my drinking. I was drinking considerably less than usual. Although I struggled with it every time I drank, I usually managed to stay under control, and only got to the point of blacking-out one or two times. And the other time, I just don't remember. For a whole three months, that was a new course record. I was on my best behavior, and maybe, just maybe, I was almost "cured."

On April 25, 2003, our last day of training when we were to be sworn in as volunteers and foreign ambassadors of the United States Government, I was hit with food poisoning and it was a relief to me. In such a time of celebration? You're damn right. It gave me an excuse not to drink. I was happier to be nauseous and sober than to go into another temporary battle at that point.

What was going on in my head was a complete reversal of thoughts. My time between graduation from college and admission into the Peace Corps (nine months) had taught me one thing: alcohol's effects on me weren't all that great anymore and I was definitely not like the rest of 'em. I was now starting to realize that, once I put that shit in my body, a little switch flipped, and it flipped noticeably to the point where there was a little fuel gauge in my head telling me I was one or two drinks shy of feeling okay. When sober and completely straightened out, I hated taking the first drink or two because I knew I was crossing over that line. It was as if I had gone through some type of aversion therapy because inside I was saying, "No, no, no," but socially and behaviorally I wanted it to be okay. Besides, I had found it more difficult to explain, lie or just say, "I can't drink," or "I'm not drinking tonight."

What kept me going back was that after a drink or four, everything was cool and I was in the clear for the next, oh, two or three hours...TOPS. From there, along with sometimes futile strategizing, it was a roll of the dice. Circumstantially, I could usually avoid loss of control or blackout, but not always. The bigger problem to me was that I could never avoid the eventual withdrawal.

Bam. I was a volunteer and out alone in my little community. But this was a good thing for me. I lived with two families, each for a month, and then on my own in a little house across the street from the school in the center of the community. I found great peace and serenity being out in the country with some of the warmest people I have ever encountered. I struggled with the indigenous language but adapted and came into my own. I helped the villagers in the fields; we picked and ate fresh fruit; and they helped me with my language and taught me their traditional ways of cooking and living. In my off time, I did all the things just mentioned, as well as spent a lot of time playing guitar and writing in my journal.

One evening I scribbled, "A long night of drinking used to make me tired...now it makes me stay up and shake." What followed was what I wrote in my first chapter. I was amazed at how much I had to say about my drinking and how easily I could recall details about how it had affected me. My insides were full of all kinds of feelings and thoughts, yet I had been very good at bottling them and storing them, so to say. That manifesto, *My Drink*, all came out in one night during my first month in my village community. It was the first time I really explored my alcohol problems.

What I noticed from that point on was how completely obsessed I was with alcohol. When I wasn't drinking during my service in South America, I was extremely happy to be sober and free of the bondage it had me under. When there was alcohol around, I did everything I could think of to avoid having it offered to me. At times, I drank a bit with a family because it was normal to them (like a lot of people) and it was almost disrespectful not to take a nip off their cheap but potent beverage. It was terrible how much premeditation went into my every move around the stuff. Of course, after two or three drinks, I could feel the buzz and would suffer later in bed either at night or in the morning depending on how much I ended up drinking. It really was not worth it to me and I was always looking for a way out of drinking.

For the most part, if it had stayed that simple for me, maybe I would have continued at that level. I could possibly have developed an understanding that I just shouldn't drink at all. *Possibly.* And then, eventually, my language level would have exceeded the level required to explain to them in the indigenous language that "Toren no like alcohol. Make him feel bad man." But that wasn't the case. I still saw other volunteers about once a month. I am in no way blaming them. The problem was simply that when I was with them, I was still trying to be something I couldn't: a social drinker. It wasn't working.

It began to affect my attitude and I started feeling hopeless. I surrendered to the idea that I'd have to tough it out and drink when I was in certain situations, inevitably enjoying the greater part of it around the other volunteers. It was always later that I'd find myself bearing the consequences of the withdrawal symptoms on my own, often wondering if maybe this time the indicators wouldn't happen. But they were always there. I would take the bus back from the city with a fever and unsettled dread about the long night and day or two ahead, in fear of a seizure or hoping that this time I'd magically sleep through the hell. I often arrived home after dark so that I could sweat it out until I had normalized enough to show myself. This caused a lot of inner struggle and a self-inflicted suffering that made me really uneasy. I thought masking it was a good idea but it only seemed to increase the feelings and scare me more.

The last four times I drank, I experienced the same progression and telltale characteristics of my binges. First, I was anxious and full of anticipation. I hoped I would find a way not to drink. Next, there was always a failing attempt to control my drinking. I didn't ever just say, "No." (That didn't make sense to me…yet.) I always wanted to participate and moderate it. I would tell myself, "Just a few drinks like the rest of them, and then turn in early so you don't suffer all night or in the morning." Well, after the first drink the switch turned on, I'd be swept away with a consistent need to maintain a level of 'just a little bit of alcohol to keep me above the line,' to keep me feeling normal. Invariably, it would result in a several day binge and I would begin replacing my food intake with alcohol.

As long as I had a few drinks, everything was fine and I could be just like the rest of them. But it wasn't sitting well on the inside and it was becoming more absurd to me. I was drinking like I had through the weekends in college, but *then* it had been for *fun* and with other people. Suddenly, I was doing it just to get by. Now I didn't bother hiding it, even though no one else was doing it with me. I continued this behavior out of necessity until I got home to my village and could go through my 'payment period' of withdrawals and could resume sober life at my site.

I knew that I would frequently be required to go to the city to meet other volunteers and that I'd be in situations where there'd be drinking. My alcoholic thinking was very stubborn. It had not occurred to me that I just had to stop drinking entirely. The disease of alcoholism seems to have a way of keeping the drinker feeling pinned down, thinking they have to drink, that there's no other way.

I had always been a hard drinker, partied hard and accepted

that if I had to die young, then so be it. At one point, I used to think aloud, "I might as well smoke, nothing else can stop me," or "Smoke a lot or not at all so you don't live to regret it." I really began to think certain things were simply inevitable. If I were suffering, it would just be part of the deal of being a hard drinker. As my brother pointed out once, it would be a self-fulfilling prophecy if I accepted this and went along with it.

At the same time as my disease worsened, I began believing this type of rationalization. My thinking had become so distorted and twisted that I'd completely lost sight of objectivity or what was normal behavior. But I knew something was wrong.

In the end, I became very worn down by the cycle of my binges. When my brother came to South America to visit me, I had planned on telling him where I was with my whole thought process and that I was looking for answers—somewhere in the back of my mind, at least. Immediately, when we met up, we had drinks with a friend and my switch was activated. I told them about my problems, but only numerous drinks later, when it became easier to talk about. It was effortless to do, in fact. I repeated it the next night as well, and it occurred to me that I was complaining about something I should be able to prevent. I felt even more stupid to find out that everything I was saying, I had already stated to them the night before. I had very little recollection of it.

My agony began to leak out when I got intoxicated enough. A month later, I repeated this scenario with a few volunteers. It was all fun and games, a whole day of maintenance drinking, until someone had to 'get crazy' with shots of vodka. That someone was me. Soon enough, I was good and blacked-out and apparently sharing the turmoil to some shocked but supportive friends. I couldn't keep it bottled up inside myself anymore. Later on, when I heard news of my confession and realized that I had worried some of them without even remembering any of it, I felt pretty fed up with myself. I wished I would either shut up or just not drink. It wasn't my job to bring the world into my head and into my fight with alcohol. It was apparent to me that I was ill and the results were beginning to spill over and get out of my control.

My blackouts increased. I started to notice a lot more unpredictability. It seemed like every time I began drinking again they were worsening and I was losing my grip or alcohol was tightening its grip on me. All I wanted was to rid myself of the problem and resume life in my community where I was at ease and happy.

I talked to one of my close volunteer friends several times about my drinking. Although I was in a state of confusion, I told him I knew I had a problem and I described the detox, how I blacked out here and there and that it was really starting to affect me. He expressed concern and asked me if I'd ever thought about quitting or drinking less. I said that I enjoyed partying and that my time wasn't up yet, but I knew that I'd have to cut down. Or maybe I'd have to stop—someday.

I'd observed how much other people drank, and how fast or how slow. I was aware that my friend drank just a few drinks and always cut himself off. I never saw him drunk but he always had fun and sometimes cut out early. He told me that he had alcoholism in his family and that his heavy drinking had run its course. He didn't like how it had affected him near the end of his partying days. So he drank very little and that was it. I really respected this guy, how he managed to limit his drinks and stuck to it. I'd been trying but couldn't. We shared the same upcoming birthday and would be meeting everyone at the All-Volunteer Conference at the beginning of the next month. It was there that I would finally give up the fight and blow my brains out, metaphorically.

15

Home Sweet unSafe Home

Drinking While Driving

...I AM HAPPY
RIDING IN A CAR WITH MY BROTHER
AND DRINKING FROM A PINT OF OLD CROW.
WE DO NOT HAVE ANY PLACE IN MIND TO GO
WE ARE JUST DRIVING.
IF I CLOSED MY EYES FOR A MINUTE
I WOULD BE LOST, YET
I COULD GLADLY LIE DOWN AND SLEEP FOREVER
BESIDE THIS ROAD.
MY BROTHER NUDGES ME.
ANY MINUTE NOW, SOMETHING WILL HAPPEN.

RAYMOND CARVER, *ALL OF US* [49]

THE VOLKMANN BROTHERS' UNWAVERING LOYALTY TO ONE ANOTHER
creates a bond that can be divided by only one thing: Paper-Rock-
Scissors. This game decides who gets the last scoop of ice cream,
who goes first off the diving board, who takes out the garbage or
who cleans up the broken vase. With only twenty months between
births, Toren and his two older brothers are close not only in years,
but in steadfast devotion. They shared the same bedroom until we
relocated to a larger house. At mid-grade school, Don and I thought
they should have their own rooms. The boys cried and argued with
us when 'required' to be separated. What resulted was, they still

spent all their free time together inventing games and adventures, playing Paper-Rock-Scissors, and parted only when it was time for lights out.

In high school and college, the three brothers negotiated a well-stocked and never-ending supply of communal friends on athletic teams, in classes, within our close-knit neighborhood and throughout community activities. Opportunities for camaraderie multiplied times three. Their best friends became universal in the sense that they spent time with any generic Volkmann brother. When kids dropped by our home, it didn't matter who was here to greet them; they shared friends unconditionally. Friendships which began in kindergarten are still in process.

'O-town,' as the brothers fondly refer to it, is Olympia, the place where these three kids grew up. We moved there when our oldest son began second grade. "*It's the Water*" is the logo of Olympia Brewery which reigned with the beer legacies of Olympia, Pabst, Schmidt's, and Miller beers; corporations that offered free tours. You could not only drink the beer there, but see how it was made. The boys often met friends at the brewery when returning to town from college where they would again take the tour (they probably could have guided it themselves) and down a free brewsky afterwards.

Lots of different boys rotated through our family, often joining us for weekend trips to a rustic family cabin on the rugged Pacific coast. There we spent hours walking the beach, running ourselves ragged climbing hogbacks, building forts and rafts, cooking outdoors, chopping firewood, playing board games under the light of a lantern and talking together about everything possible. Don and I had the unique opportunity to be thrown in the midst of these kids over a span of twenty years as they spent this expansive time with us. Because the cabin is one room and completely isolated from development, the boys and their friends were forced to interact with us. The hours spent driving there in our jam-packed Suburban, pitching in for chores and beach excursions, and talking together in front of a crackling fire with no other agenda provided many memories. If we had not had this chance to know the boys' friends so thoroughly, perhaps I would feel more jaded upon learning the extent of Toren's infatuation with alcohol and parties. But I have seen both sides. I have seen both the Safe and the unSafe, the tentative morphing of boys into men.

It may be difficult for Toren when he emerges from rehab since he and his brothers share the same dangerous DNA, along with a composite of party memories and a posse of mutual buddies. I wonder how they will socialize with Toren when he is unable to consume alcohol and whether or not he will choose to see them.

After Toren's startling revelation to our family, his brothers check out the rehab website for themselves. They call to ask what we've heard from him. I inform them about Toren's recent letter from rehab, his battle with the Higher Power. I don't tell them what the therapist said, that Toren's own brothers could be hazardous for him. That maybe Toren shouldn't be around them for awhile because they 'used' together. "They drink a lot?" she'd asked me for verification. But it was really more of a declaration.

That reminds me of the wallet I've kept hidden away on the top shelf of my closet. Inside are about fifteen fake I.D.s used by the boys, some with each other's names, friends' names, even one with the name of one of Don's friends. They're from diverse states, but they all have pictured one son or another. As I took them away from the boys throughout the years, I stockpiled them together. I'd thought that someday we could pull them out and laugh. But not now; it's not so funny.

When the boys came home from college in summertime, they stayed close, packing lunches for one another and sharing rides to work. At one point they stretched a long cord from bedroom-to-bedroom, tied to each of their wrists, which they pulled in the mornings to be sure they would wake on time. On weekends, they divided up friends and social invitations. If one brother had something to celebrate, any number of friends would show up to join in, spread within a range of five to six years. Our family did a lot of burgers, boating, and sports tournaments with the boys and their friends. We incorporated them into our family and treated them as our own.

One Monday morning in the summer after Toren's freshman

year of college, Toren did not get up to go to work. When I returned to the house around noon, he was still in bed. I could tell he was hung over, and we had a long talk about it. "Toren," I warned him, "if you're too hung over to go to work, it's a red flag. You need to pay attention to your partying, because this is a sign of alcohol problems." Toren had great difficulty responding, but he knew I was serious. He scrambled out of bed and didn't let it happen again. Now I wonder how he managed it. Little did I know.

What made our home 'unSafe'? Probably the fact that we were so happy to have the boys back, we didn't challenge their social habits enough. Our house is ten miles out of town, and we preferred the boys not drive home after drinking alcohol. For this reason they often stayed in town with friends on weekends. We also figured that since they were now in college, they could set their own hours, as long as they had steady jobs, respected our home, and helped out when needed. We wanted them to manage their own time.

Toren and his brothers attended extended family events, worked at their grandparents' house, and visited Don's father across the mountains. They helped us with projects. We enjoyed having them around. When some of the boys' college friends dropped by to visit, they called me "VolkMom" and recalled times we'd seen them on campus. Some of these students were Triceptatrough seniors. No wonder they liked us.

"You Volkmann Bros have the coolest parents," they said. Right. We found out how easily it went down; we sold out. Look at what we learned.

That incident aside, probably the most palpable danger at the home of the Perfect Family is the ability for the brothers to get into mischief together, to set one another off. Who can jump off the highest cliff? Who can eat the greasiest hamburgers? Out-drinking one another could be a contest as well. Later on, Paper-Rock-Scissors determines designated drivers. And when a brother nudges a brother, it means something *is* important, whether happening now or about to happen; or even if it's never happened. That's why our Perfect Family lives in a Home Sweet unSafe Home. The coalition of brothers keeps the walls glued together in tight unity. Nothing can crack it.

And normal things? Normal is a myth. Our family is ready to discuss a new definition of us. Now that we've unearthed the Volkmann Genetic Blueprint, our sons are looking at Home somewhat differently. When they return here after Toren has finished rehab someday, we know it won't be the same. Already, when we phone one another, it's changed. We're all talking about alcohol, how much we're drinking, how much we used to drink, if we should, can we never?

"What could I have done to prevent this?" I ask the older two on the phone.

"You did great, Mom," they assure me.

"Maybe I could have instructed him better...."

"Program Toren?" They laugh at me. "Mom, he's grown up. He makes his own decisions. You're free after graduation. On your own, like Toren was in the Peace Corps." He was beginning his life.

What has our 'You're on your Own after College Graduation' plan done for our kids? Where did it get them—those brewery head boys we raised. All those dinners together, mountain hikes, family times with grandparents, reading *City of Joy* as a family, symphony concerts together. I wonder if it helped. Sure thing, we shouldn't have bought those kegs for the first two boys' college graduations. By the time Toren graduated, we said, NO MORE BIG PARTIES. Because maybe we knew. Maybe we saw the UNsafety of our home: a finality of success and graduation with three tuitions paid off, the relaxed thinking. We thought it was all lined up. Now, we pay the real price.

I gather the clues in order, things I think that we missed seeing. If I were a parent telling another parent how to make home Safer, I'd say, "Look out!" Because here's what we neglected:

- ✓ Seeing or learning about our son being intoxicated in public and not signing up for professional counseling. (This could have been addressed in high school.)
- ✓ Allowing our high school-aged son to visit college campuses without being accompanied by a parent. (Some kids may be mature enough to do this, but we should have known better with Toren.)

- ✓ Seeing our son laying or sitting around breaking a sweat for no reason.
- ✓ Seeing our son trembling sometimes.
   (We did ask him about it, but he said he wasn't feeling well; we believed him.)
- ✓ Not knowing exactly where our son was during some of his college vacations; leaving too much unstructured time on his spring breaks.
   (It would seem a responsible college kid could handle this on his own. Too much hand-holding wasn't our style, but in this case we were remiss.)
- ✓ Seeing our son in legal difficulty as a result of alcohol use and not pursuing counseling.
   (We told him to handle his own problems, but did not aid him in dealing with the cause of his difficulties.)
- ✓ Not working out a secure, structured plan for immediate post-college graduation.
   (We thought we had this covered with Toren's eminent plans for language school in Mexico and ensuing Peace Corps employment, but Toren's plan was to party and drink . We thought it was to find a job and take care of himself. He did find a summer job in Seattle before leaving for Mexico, and somehow he functioned well enough to get by, at least on the surface. His time spent in Las Vegas was obviously frivolous. Our downfall was that we ignored his extensive partying. Since he didn't live with us, we were unaware of its pervasiveness.)
- ✓ Repeating over again any of the above mistakes and trying to rationalize it.

After writing these guidelines, I show them to Toren. (By the time he reads them, he's finished his rehab and is living in a halfway program.) He comments that no matter what we'd have done, he probably wouldn't have cooperated until he was good and ready. He says that our efforts may have been wasted had we pursued any of the above avenues. Jokingly, Toren suggests he needed intervention even *before* he drank one drop.

"But what about the D.A.R.E. program you had in middle school?" I ask him.

"That was too soon." He explains, "The information was good to have, like all the facts I was presented, but I didn't think it applied to me. And I didn't care about it."

"And what about intervention after college?"

"By then, it was almost too late."

Never too late, I think to myself. "What about counseling in high school?"

"It might've worked, but I probably would've thought my problem wasn't that serious." He goes on to say, "I had to have enough time to make a pile of bad decisions in order to realize I had a problem with alcohol. The only way to find out I had a problem was to let it manifest itself. You can't intervene too soon."

When to interrupt the abuse is the key question. But I keep thinking, "What if…?" Maybe, by me saying this, some other parents will have the courage or foresight to make an attempt.

Now in our home, empty of boys, my husband and I look at our own usage of alcohol and our lifestyle. We've been known to go out dancing with our sons, to accompany them to sports bars or to receptions where alcohol is served. Alcohol has not been central to our family activities. Yet, it was there. As we face an addicted family member, we scrutinize our home differently. What used to be reassuring appears threatening; there's a shadow hanging over our front door. Our patterns have become disrupted. But perhaps it's for the better. We thought Paper-Rock-Scissors was a thing of the past. At this point we realize, "Any minute now, something will happen."

16

Nothing Social About It

On the evening of September 11, 2003, all regional Peace Corps Volunteers met in the capital city for a conference focused on upcoming events, goals, and coordination of volunteers with varied skills to work together in cross-sector projects. Following this meeting, many newer volunteers, including myself, invited a representative from their individual communities to join us for two more days in a Project Design and Management Workshop. This meant a six-day stretch of extremely helpful idea-sharing and a great opportunity to get to know all of the other volunteers. I was aware that alcohol would be around and wanted to limit my drinking, and participate without any craziness. I wanted the results to reflect work that I knew I could do when I was sober and able to do things right. I had very good intentions but, unfortunately, I still hadn't realized that control and drinks didn't belong in the same arena for me.

The first night was fine. I would have chosen not to even drink or had 'just a few.' But because it was my birthday, I thought I'd let it slide a bit. It was satisfactory and I did the whole next day with minimal side effects. However, the switch *had* been flipped and by early that afternoon the deal was pretty much sealed. I'd be drinking again soon. Every time my sobriety was broken, it seemed easier to keep sliding down in social situations. I chose to drink rather than walk uphill the hard way to get out of the situation. Avoiding alcohol to bypass withdrawals and feel better no longer worked for me. It was easier to continue drinking than to stop and detox.

I knew I was gonna drink that next night. No matter what, it'd already started. And I did. Like usual, it began earlier, I drank a lot more, and it went a lot later. I made two late-night runs to the store for boxes of wine, but it was only because we were having such a great time and I didn't want it to end. I knew that more drinks would keep it going; at least it would for me. I could have gone on drinking all night. At least it felt that way and my body said I could.

The next morning I woke up sleeping in a bed on the other side of the facility in a different sleeping quarter. I had completely blacked out and a few of us had slept through the morning lectures. Normally I wouldn't care, but I was already fed up with this shit, and that pissed me off. Unpredictable. The night had been a blast all the way to the moment I pulled a disappearing act from my memory. To remedy the effects, I drank a lot of water. I had some pretty bad shakes and tremors and noticed that food was starting to seem foreign to me. That afternoon, I was able to appear normal and enjoy myself, but still, my thoughts were completely preoccupied with when I could get to the next drink. I may have been there physically but my mind was out to 'lunch'—with drinks.

At this point, I realized I was at a crossroads. I had two options. I could either fight it and suffer a pretty nauseating withdrawal and eventually recuperate after tremendous discomfort and another long night or two, or I could continue to drink and put off the problem and act as if everything was normal. My rational alcoholic mind gave me no choice.

"Yeah, right, you're not putting yourself through that now or tonight." Besides, all the volunteers would be at a bar that night and I was already wet in my mind. I also knew that my community representative, Lucio, loved to drink. This meant that while he was with us I wouldn't have to withdraw; I could just keep up the momentum and make it through. It was an ugly situation but I was running out of options. My sense of humor and reason were both by the wayside at this point. By continuing to drink, in my brilliance, I was avoiding pain and solving the problem. Temporarily.

The third night at the bar I drank 'slow and steady' because I didn't want to black out and lose it all like I'd apparently done the night before—neither the control nor my memory. What I didn't realize was that my control was already gone when I picked up my first drink. What a joker. By the end of the night, I'd maintained a pretty consistent feeling of intoxication.

I noticed that as my disease progressed, walking the fine line of maintaining myself between withdrawal, over-intoxication or blacking out for an extended period of time was increasingly difficult and dangerous. You need X amount of alcoholic drinks in your system to feel normal or a little good, like most normal people or moderate drinkers feel. But if you get to another plateau a bit further along, you begin to let all your guards down, which is still normal. Unfortunately, there is another part to the alcoholic system that tells you, "Yes, yes!! This is it. Keep doing this; it's working!" And, somewhere in there, you go from a normal buzz to a heavy buzz (and keep drinking while thinking everything is cool) to gone. You don't remember it, but you may be 'around' for hours more, and often the drinking accelerates. According to some, a real blackout artist can lose days or more. It is a terrible feeling to have no clue about what you missed. Attempting to appear like you know what happened the night before, you have to play detective to figure it out.

When I met my community representative Lucio at the bus terminal on the fourth day, I'd already had two beers to take the edge off. Afterall, I felt good. But I realized how ridiculous it was. Basically, for the next two-and-a-half days I struggled to keep my urges to drink at bay. I was at a loss for how to do this. I had completely lost sight of:

Why I was at the conference,

What I had intended to do,

What really mattered,

What I wanted,

What I was supposed to be doing for my community.

All I could think about was drinking when my system got low. I didn't consider it a craving; *it was a physical necessity.* Before my eyes, I had watched my will completely deteriorate over the duration of six days. I had compromised everything for alcohol. It was my new priority. And this was the first time that there was *nothing* social about it. Not one other volunteer was drinking with me. I started leaving in the middle of lectures or activities to gather myself, get fresh air or strategize. It was moment-to-moment until my avoidance no longer postponed what I saw as inevitable. My next drink.

I knew that about ten blocks away was the same store I'd gone to before. I also understood that two or three drinks would stop the suffering and shut it all off, returning me to feeling normal and functional, the only things I really wanted. At that point, I didn't care. I had to do what was necessary for me, so I could get past my craving and back to participating in the conference.

I went to the store, disgusted with myself, but at the same time relieved that I could at least end the problem. On the way back from the liquor store, walking through a ritzy neighborhood, I encountered a horse and buggy. I did something I never thought I would: I took a ride in it. I felt bad about this because all the other volunteers were doing what they were supposed to be doing. Not me. But it sure was fun.

When I returned to the conference I downed my few drinks, even though they tasted like varnish or worse. I attempted to rejoin the normal folks. Very few knew that I had left to get alcohol, and even less about my horse and buggy adventure. I was pretty good at faking things at this point.

I was now completely aware that I had lost the battle and was closer to the stereotypical closet drinker. I had reached a new low in my book. My will was broken. I was hiding drinks and actually ashamed for the first time. I believe I was more scared about what was going on than I'd ever been before, but there was no way in hell I was ready to bring another volunteer into my poisoned world. I chose this sordid path and it was my deal. A drink was always the cure to ignore the problem.

Towards the end of the conference, things got pretty blurry to me. The only thing I know with any reliability is that any time my fuel level was low I would drink a bit to 'keep it under control.' What finally urged me to go to the nurse's office at headquarters still baffles me. I don't remember a definitive moment where I said to myself, "This is it. I'm turning you in," or anything like that.

But I do remember one foot in front of the other, up those steps, through the door and sitting down in a chair facing the desk and staring blankly. The same nurse had driven me to the terminal three days before and had smelled alcohol on me then. Everyone must have known I smelled like alcohol except me. From this point on, I began to feel relief and comfort because I was able to talk about what was up and get it out of my swelling head. After my score tallied more points than were possible on a question-and-answer test for alcoholism, it was now just as clear to her that I had a problem.

From this point on, all possible procedural steps were taken to get me back to Washington, D.C., ASAP, where I could be properly helped by the best of professionals. Uh, oh. What had I done? I was given Valium and put in a hotel room to detox in the care of some of my good Peace Corps friends.

This detox for me was not a usual one. Normally, I bore it all alone and if people were around, I never told them what I was feeling inside: the almost inexplicable discomfort—which was always there. But this time with Valium, the withdrawal effects were subtle and nearly undetectable. It was also the first time I'd made anyone aware of what I was going through.

From the doctor's office, the nurse called my friends at the hotel and asked them, "Have you ever been around anyone coming off alcohol?" She then explained the seriousness of it and that they'd have to get rid of all the alcohol in the hotel room, that they should monitor my Valium intake, and that I'd be sweating a lot. Although they didn't realize it, they'd been hanging around with me long enough that they definitely had witnessed someone coming off alcohol. Only now, it had been formally acknowledged. We managed to have a good time in spite of the underlying darkness of what the situation really meant. Beneath the smiles and conversation, there was sadness about what I was going through. Many said conciliatory things and that they were proud of me, but nobody knew it was really time to say good-bye.

The next afternoon I was driven to my site to pack some items for Washington, D.C., a trip that I figured would last a week or two, tops. Still on my Valium detox plan with my friends in the capital city two-and-one-half hours away, I absentmindedly threw some CDs together, got my guitar, and pulled out some clothing that would not be sufficient for the unforeseen fall temperatures at rehab.

As for the trip to Washington, D.C. ...Well, I'm still on it.

Thankfully, before leaving my village in South America, I got to briefly see my two families and my buddy Lucio, who had witnessed some of my struggles and desperation in my final days. I had no idea that I was leaving the place permanently and that those were my final good-byes to the community and all the volunteers. And maybe, those were also my good-byes to drinking. Believe it or not, the last one is the hardest to comprehend for a drunk like me.

17

CALLS FROM REHAB

LET HER
FALL IN LOVE WITH YOU AND YOU
WITH HER AND THEN. . .SOMETHING: ALCOHOL,
A PROBLEM WITH ALCOHOL, ALWAYS ALCOHOL-
WHAT YOU'VE REALLY DONE
AND TO SOMEONE ELSE, THE ONE
YOU MEANT TO LOVE FROM THE START.

RAYMOND CARVER, *ALCOHOL, ALL OF US* [50]

SUNDAY, 5 OCTOBER 2003. FINALLY, AFTER OVER EIGHT DAYS, WE RECEIVE our first phone call from Toren. He has survived the initial week of rehab, supposedly the toughest. I listen to his voice for the tone, his inflections, for any indication of his mood. He sounds thoughtful, focused. There is noise in the background because he must use a phone located where visitors are received, a period which extends for two hours on Sundays. A baby cries in the background. I picture people chatting and laughing amidst friends and relatives, but Toren alone. He speaks clearly, "I'm working on acceptance of the cost of my alcoholism. This week was intense." He mentions quickly the haunting trio of Anger, Guilt, and Shame. "I know now that I'm worse off than I thought. I'm going to do whatever they say," Toren confesses.

It must have been grueling. The person speaking doesn't sound like the guy I talked to over seven days ago. His voice is level and he doesn't seem discouraged when he admits, "I might have to leave

South America for good."

"That's not what you wanted," I suggest.

"The worst part is, I didn't have closure with my village. I left without explaining things. That is so hard for me to deal with."

"What will you do next," I ask, "after rehab?"

"I can hardly think more than one day at a time. I just do today. But they're saying I might consider living in a halfway house, that this is what would be good." He stops here.

"Well, what do you think about that?" I ask, recalling how a halfway house once reared its prefabricated siding in our former neighborhood. That'd been almost twenty years ago. And I'd joined with other neighbors to lobby against it ("I just don't want my children associating with that type of person," I'd justified). Then I'd signed a Not-In-My-Back-Yard! (NIMBY) letter. Now *my* kid is talking about going to some town to live in one. I'm immediately grateful to those citizens if they'll give him this chance. I know Toren will be nice to his neighbors. I feel guilty while I continue talking to my son.

"I'm not enthused. It's not appealing," he says, "but I'm here to listen to what they tell me." His voice has lost the early fervor of the call. It takes on a slightly forced tone, one of resignation, somewhat hopeless.

It took courage for Toren to turn himself in and admit he had a problem when he was so enamored with his life in South America. He'd had to give it up. I remember he'd said he wouldn't have come forward if he'd known they would yank him out of his service. What if he'd died in the jungle? I shudder; maybe a halfway house isn't such a bad alternative. It would give Toren organization for his life, a positive spin. Hopefully he wouldn't run into any disapproving NIMBYs like me.

"If you live in a halfway house, you'll have structure," I say reassuringly. "You'll be able to relax because temptation will be out of sight." I look at Toren's free time after college graduation, where it had put him. I had disliked his choices then and suddenly this halfway house doesn't sound so bad.

The phone call changes pace when Toren asks if we know about the Family Education Program. I hear someone hacking away at a cough in the background as I tell him we're planning to come, in fact just that day I'd been working on flight arrangements.

"You and Dad?" he asks.

"Yes, and your brothers, too."

"OH, LORD."

"What?" I'm not sure what Toren is trying to tell me.

"You said the whole family's coming? Oh, Lord," he repeats. Then he spills out, "It's going to rip our family apart. You'll have to write letters to me telling me how I've hurt you. I don't want anyone to feel betrayed, to feel like they have to 'sign up'—to change their lives because of me." Toren sounds panicked. "I thought you and Dad might come, but my brothers? Are you sure they can come?"

"Yes, I've called them, and they're clearing their schedules. They both had conflicts on Thursday, but they'll fly out on Friday in time to be there Saturday morning. We've checked out flights already."

"Our family's going to have to be honest," Toren warns. He's worrying about us, about his brothers being coerced into attending. I wonder if there might be some other reason he's so concerned. Toren comments that one of his brothers wrote him a letter trying to be sensitive. "I think coming here will really affect them because you have to be honest about yourself in regards to what you want in your life and how actively you're going after it. I don't want my brothers to feel threatened about their drinking, but this could be hard for them."

I tell Toren that this weekend symposium will be good for all of us. "We have to live together (hopefully) a long time, Toren, and if we can't be honest, then we won't have a good relationship."

"Our family's probably the healthiest family they'll ever see here in rehab," Toren comments. "Really, it'll be embarrassing. Everyone has anger, shame, guilt and anxiety issues. But the education program will cause our family to be more open with each other." Toren resigns himself.

He goes on to tell me that he has been worrying not only about how his brothers will react to him, but what his longtime friends will do when they hear the news. He thinks that only a few buddies would be able to understand him never drinking again. "I might have to give up a lot of my former friends. I don't know how and when to tell people."

I suggest that Toren talk with his therapist about his brothers and his friends and he agrees it's a good idea. It seems strange for me to be slinging around the term 'your therapist' so casually with my son like something out of an old Woody Allen movie.

Then I ask Toren if he has been receiving my cards and letters. He tells about opening his mail in front of the guard, a hardened man who has seen everything and is notoriously stoic on the job. But Toren got a smile out of him when he showed him an old photo I'd sent of the brothers as kids.

Toren comments on the family alcohol history sent to him by Don, how it surprised him. "I'm really astounded by all the alcoholics in the family. Did you know about it?" he asks. I tell him it was startling to me as well.

Toren continues saying, "I'm constantly busy here. There's hardly time to make a phone call." He explains that there're a lot of lectures and group discussions but downtime, particularly Sunday, is slow because he can't be alone. He is required to be interacting with someone and to remain in public. The only reading material is the *Big Book* (AA material). "It's hard to sit here blindly not knowing what to do or what I will be doing in the immediate future. I don't know what to prepare for."

I ask Toren what he wants from us, for us to do.

He says, "Feel good for me. Don't feel bad or sad."

So I try to do that. I will myself to cheer up. After all, I *am* proud of him, of his brutal honesty. The rest of the week I'm busy renting a car, finding a hotel, and facilitating arrivals at the airport near Toren's rehab facility. Gretchen, Toren's therapist calls to ask if I have any questions about the weekend program and Toren's progress. She casually brings up the halfway house and I do not tell her about my former negative attitude. She tells me that the aftercare team is looking into good placement options for Toren.

Aftercare. I think about the stigma of telling friends that my son's living in a halfway house. That sounds humiliating enough, but the feedback from Toren's brothers is even more quizzical.

"I think they're overreacting with this rehab program," one of his brothers tells me. "Yeah, I've had the shakes. Are they going to enroll me now? And this halfway house stuff, isn't that for addicts?" (Yes, son, it is.)

Now I realize why we need Family Education. Like much of the population, Toren's brother hardly considers alcoholism an addiction. It's sort of 'an unfortunate situation.' But an addiction? Isn't that label a bit serious? Lots of people drink too much, after all. It's an accepted norm of society. We don't have to saddle them with the title of addiction, do we? It's so much easier to say 'alcohol problem' than 'alcohol addiction.' It sounds better.

Family Education seems like a seminar custom-built for us. After all, we're the near Perfect Nuclear Family (even though sociologists say the nuclear family hardly exists anymore.) Two still-married parents: an endangered species. And two sons willing to support an addicted brother: unflappable. Other addicts may not be so lucky as to have such resources for battling addiction. In reality, our family dilemma may not be so ground-breaking; the erroneous past of traditional American values has always included alcoholism. Millions of families have been in crisis and flux over the last two centuries, and our family is another example of the exploding myth. According to family scholar Stephanie Coontz, no single type of household has ever protected Americans from social disruption.[51]

With Toren being far away and rehabbing in secret, I miss being able to talk with close friends about what is happening to our family. There is a tremendous lack of support for me and my husband. At the same time, I know this disease is not all about me, it's about Toren. At least that's what I think at this point. I will later be told that alcoholism not only takes down the alcoholic, but the entire family. That's the logical reason that I'm in such turmoil. But at this point, without resources and help, I am frankly slipping into a whirlpool of panic. I lack emotional control when talking to people because I don't yet know enough about this disease. After Toren's phone, call I hit the Al-Anon website in near hysteria; I look for information on the Internet about drinking. But what I really need is someone who will talk with me about our son, someone who knows him and is working with him.

Two days later, Toren again phones. He finally announces to Don and me that he has given up returning to South America. His voice is resolute and victorious. "I've accepted it," he proclaims. "I've been through denial, anger, and now acceptance." Toren says he stood in front of the group just that day and announced that he wouldn't be going back. He says it felt good to share it.

Don and I discuss with Toren the advantages of living in a halfway house, of being with people who are clean and sober. Toren's still trying to decide where to do his halfway stint. Much of the country is off limits to him since he "used" in practically every western state. Toren is considering several eastern locations. He will find work; there are options. Toren likes his therapist and says she's cool. It's a relief to us that there is someone out there who's able to discuss things with Toren, subjects that were impossible for us to bring up. Toren says that immediately after rehab he will go to Washington, D.C., for closure with the Peace Corps. After that, he will remain three to six months at the halfway house. He doesn't know about finances, but stresses that he wants to do this on his own. He had saved summer employment funds in his bank account and feels this will get him by until he can find a job.

After Toren hangs up, I want to ask him if he can manage, if he needs us to help him move. But inside, I know that he has previously relocated to a foreign country and unfamiliar village culture on his own. Finding his spot in an American town should be relatively simple in comparison. Before we have time to comprehend all that Toren has told us, his therapist telephones. She checks on our visiting arrangements, our arrival times, and talks about setting an appointment for our family to work with the education team. She reports that Toren is doing very well and is beginning to understand his problem. Gretchen says the letter Don sent about our family alcohol history is excellent and shows outstanding support for Toren. She is working with Toren to narrow down his halfway selection to three choices. Again, she stresses that Toren should not be near his brothers. He needs to do this move on his own to prove himself because he was floundering after college. He was not making good decisions about drinking; he was all over the place.

We talk about support for Toren and whether Don and I should help him in the transition. Gretchen suggests, "Tell Toren you want to be there for him and ask him what you can do. Ask Toren to tell you if it gets to be too much." She says that Toren processes things internally and doesn't tell people what he needs. "He solves everyone else's problems but doesn't take care of himself. It's something I talked with Toren about today."

I tell her, "I'm concerned Toren won't tell us if he's unable to function because look at how he's hidden things from us before!"

Gretchen reminds me that Toren is learning to go to people when he needs help. I now remember during Toren's phone call, that he mentioned appreciation for sharing some of his burden with the group. Maybe he can do that with us.

Life seems to be a story. I wonder if Toren knows he can direct his own.

Before Toren left for the Peace Corps, I had wanted to ask him if he had any regret for his misconduct (only the things I knew about at that point). I needed to verify the real Toren: my son, the kid who had treated me so well, the boy who talked to me about injustice, world causes, and sonnets. Many times, it seemed his acting out hadn't matched the person I knew at home.

I remember the day before he departed, we crossed a rainy Costco parking lot on our way to pick up his eyeglass prescription. The glasses had to be ordered and barely arrived in time; the following day, Toren would launch himself into his South American mission. I believed he had joined the Peace Corps to contribute to the betterment of the world. Now I wanted him to convince me that he had finally realized the negative impact of certain past actions. (In my mind, I was rectifying the intelligent, thoughtful young man I knew. Who was he? Although a son who had often pushed limits, hopefully he was not as self-effacing as he'd sometimes portrayed.) Obviously, he was now ready to turn over a new chapter in his life, one of responsibility and leadership.

Trying to keep it casual, I asked him, "Do you regret any of your behavior in high school and college?" We continued towards the store entrance, plodding through random puddles, cigarette butts, and dented latte lids. He looked at me as though he couldn't understand why I would ask such an obvious thing. I rephrased it, "Do you think your life has been more difficult because of your decisions?"

Toren answered me, "No, my life's been good. I wouldn't give up my experiences."

"Even when you got into trouble?"

"Yes. Even then." He remained resolute.

Does Toren believe that way now? How good has it really been?

...and then...something: alcohol,
a problem with alcohol, always alcohol -
what you've really done
and to someone else, the one
you meant to love from the start.

18

Visiting Hours

12 October 2003. His voice is clear and strong, even cheerful. "I now know how much help I need," Toren tells us. "I'm in the hands of whatever my therapists recommend. So I'll do a halfway house three months, maybe six." The next time we hear from Toren, he announces with conviction that he'll be going to a halfway program in Florida. He sounds like he wants to settle in; become accountable. And sober. He says he was tempted by New York City, but no programs there were recommended by his treatment center. He doesn't know yet where in Florida he'll be and asks us to bring some clothes for temperate weather when we come to Family Education Weekend. Toren reads me a list of things he will need since most of his belongings are still in South America. We're allowed to deliver them to the rehab facility where they will be stored until he has finished his treatment; the program does not want anyone smuggling in unauthorized "stuff."

Toren's take is upbeat. We decide that I'll bring him a duffel bag. He requests long-sleeved shirts, a hooded sweatshirt, swim shorts, khaki pants, his flannel pants, some collared shirts, his favorite old wind breaker, and a beanie hat from the bottom of his sock drawer that says "Alcoholics" on it....I wonder what he will do with it? He also wants his drum pad.

Toren's full of news. He says he performed a song on his guitar at the rehab chapel for some two hundred people, a song he wrote himself. He sang and played the guitar. Toren is enthused about the priests there and their message to addicts. He goes on to say he likes his mail, especially letters he's received in Spanish and letters from volunteers and staff in South America. Toren's articulation is lucid and cogent. It makes me realize that it hasn't been that way for awhile. I think we're seeing him truly sober for the first time in years.

I spend the next evening packing things for Toren. I include an article on how to make a budget, an envelope with Mandala Tibetan sand and blessing music, some mints and, along with his requested favorite clothes, some new shirts, socks, and shorts. It's reassuring to get out his clothing, to see it and think that he will be wearing it sober. Sober. What a wonderful word!

I wonder if he needs more luggage. Toren left us nine months prior carrying one suitcase and a backpack. We have no idea what things he's brought back to the U.S. on unexpected notice. Those "things" aren't incredibly important. It's so much more essential for him to possess his health, his sanity, his wits, his courage to carry on: his fire to be the best person he can. Toren is fortunate at this moment to have people guiding him who care about him and know what is best for people with an alcohol addiction.

I'm thankful I can finally follow someone's direction to take care of this progressive disease, the malaise that overtook our family the past nine years. Just placing things in a suitcase seems a positive step and fills me with hope. We leave tomorrow for the Family Education Weekend. I don't even care how hokey the name sounds. I want to get smart, to learn about this thing that has happened to Toren and our family. I'm weary of feeling overwhelmed.

Before leaving, I phone Toren's brothers to remind them they cannot wear torn jeans or logo shirts to the rehab facility. This is one rule amidst other policies which ensures the safety of the patients. It's the first time I realize that ordinary symbols of drugs and alcohol, product brands or rock band names, even certain clothing styles, can be triggers for relapse. The staff at the rehab center tries to prevent clients from experiencing unnecessary anxiety when visitors unthinkingly wear something that might remind them of their addiction.

The brothers go over meeting arrangements with me. Both of them are adjusting study and work schedules to make this trip.

They've agreed to attend because I asked them. They adore their brother; if he reaches out for help, they want to be there for him. Still, I sense they cannot understand why it's *so* necessary to have the whole family with Toren. We have not been together as a family for over nine months, so even though this venture is laced with dubious speculation, we can't help but look forward to seeing one another.

I am somewhat nervous, knowing we must meet with persons who could easily see through us, who will be evaluating our family and who probably know quite a bit about us prior to our arrival since they've been working with Toren for almost three weeks now. My emotions thin, I wonder how I will hold up even with my family at my side; all my fears and joys mesh into one slobbery knot. It isn't the most calming image.

En route to the rehab facility, I'm on my own because Don and Toren's brothers are unable to break away until Friday evening. The Airporter arrives for me on Thursday morning at 5:00 a.m. under a downpour. The Pacific Northwest autumn mood wears a dour grey patina as I board the van joining two women inside, one going to Arizona to meet her high school girlfriends for a spa reunion, the other dressed for an ecology business conference in Jasper, Canada. They chatter on in lively banter about their plans as though it were three in the afternoon. When they ask where I'm going, I tell them the name of the state.

"Do you have business there?" the ecology girl asks.

 "No, my son's there."

Then the other, the one who just loved high school, wants to know, "Is he a student?"

"Yes." A student of alcohol. My emotions rush to my face and I'm grateful for the darkness of predawn. It's too early for conversation. They recognize that I must not be a morning person. I'm not talking.

There's plenty of time to adjust to what I'm about to do. Six hours on the plane and the ensuing drive in a rental car allow me to prepare for meeting our son while I ponder the relentless scripted captions which run through the skulls of all mothers, like: if Toren's had a recent haircut, if he will be lean from readjusting his diet, if he will still have his sparkle and bounce, if he will be happy to see me or embarrassed, whether he has a warm enough jacket.

I find my way to the location of the coffee hour where we are scheduled to meet other family support members who will be spending the weekend with us. This is taxing for me because, with my directional dyslexia, I can barely find my way around my own neighborhood, let alone driving through a foreign state to a rambling rehab center with hazily-labeled buildings and other lost-looking people. But I do it. There's a sense that I'm not really here, not really carrying out this mission. It's nothing I'd imagined doing; no dream come true. When I enter the meeting room, I immediately sense that neither is it a fantasy visit for the other twenty or so people in attendance. We all look miserable, like we may have been sent there for detention. Eye contact is nil.

But rehab centers are expert at what they do. And their purpose this weekend is not to humiliate us. All of us are here because we care deeply for someone in treatment. As the morning passes, we begin to recognize that. We all want to experience some form of success and understanding with our family members. It occurs to me that other people are not so pleased to be seeing their loved ones as I am to be seeing Toren. In fact, some appear to dread it; others look reasonably angry. I try to hide how excited I am to get my arms around my son.

The first day of the program is devoted largely to education about addiction, about the disease of alcoholism and about the role of the family in relation to the alcoholic. The presentations are dynamic and informative. I take notes. It's fascinating to me. I realize that this disease has tracked down my son and ravaged his brain in the same relentless manner that threatens 20 percent of our population. My son is not alone in his addiction. But he is one of the lucky ones: he has sought help.

Apparently, I'm one of 80 percent of the population who is able to drink alcohol. Our facilitator explains that such social drinkers regulate their drinking, perhaps after a few bad experiences with alcohol, and can continue to do so throughout their lives. But the other 20 percent face alcohol abuse or addiction. And as I learn from other participating family members, this disease is non-discriminating. It selects people from all walks of life. It leads even those of strong and good character into its clutches. And the despair it creates surrounds me in the meeting room that morning.

The most interesting part of the presentation is the discussion of addiction. An accepted definition of addiction: The repetitive, compulsive use of a substance despite negative consequences to the user.[52] Addiction features three or more of these seven characteristics:

1. Increased tolerance
2. Withdrawal
3. Attempts to cut down or control use
4. Use despite adverse social or personal consequences
5. Use despite physical or psychological harm
6. Large quantities of time and effort and money spent on obtaining substance
7. Substance taken in larger quantities or for longer amounts of time than intended

The disease of alcoholism, like other diseases such as heart disease or diabetes, is treatable. The goal of the rehab staff is to allow people to die *with* their addiction instead of *from* their addiction. Cost to U.S. society for consequences of alcohol use alone is staggering, approximately $1000 per individual who consumes alcohol. In terms of morbidity and mortality, the years a drinker loses to alcoholic liver disease is 10 years compared to 2 years from cancer and 4 years from heart disease.[53]

Why does an addict keep using? The reward circuit of the brain craves a substance called dopamine, and such things as food, sex, or addictive drugs (alcohol included) produce the release of dopamine. Scientists are just now realizing the strong role of dopamine in addiction and how the brain and body adapt to levels of dopamine production.[54] Alcohol drinking increases the release of dopamine in the reward centers of the brain. Studies show that the increase in dopamine activity occurs only while the concentration of alcohol in the blood is rising, not while it is falling.

So during the first moments after drinking, the pleasure circuits in the brain are activated. But the dopamine "rush" disappears after the alcohol level stops rising. This may motivate the drinker to consume more alcohol in order to start the pleasure sequence again, called "chasing the high." The problem is that although the rush is over, there is still plenty of alcohol in the body and continued drinking in pursuit of pleasure signals could push the blood alcohol concentration up to dangerous levels.[55] When dopamine quantities in the brain level off, the addict is no longer able to sustain enough of the chemical to relieve withdrawal symptoms. Then the body and brain demand the chemical (alcohol) to stop withdrawal symptoms, and the addict is no longer using the drug for pleasure, but to relieve pain and the unpleasant effects of withdrawal. It makes the alcoholic feel anxious and restless, to crave the drug.

Actual experiments using an MRI of the brain have measured levels of dopamine produced when an addict receives a drug of choice. On these films, it's possible to observe how brain patterns change physiologically and how neural circuits are modified by chronic use of alcohol or drugs. Since the human brain is not fully formed until late in adolescence, it's possible that heavy drug use can alter that development. Studies are still being run in this area. From what I learn in this class, I realize what has happened in Toren's brain, and I better understand his increased use of alcohol.

Now I see how addiction and control are two opposite concepts. By the time Toren cultivated his taste for alcohol and experienced the enhanced levels of dopamine, his brain never looked back. When modification of his neural circuits took over, good sense was blotted out with the overriding desire for dopamine.

With my head full of lingo and my notebook crammed with facts, I'm finally allowed to meet with Toren. We rendezvous in the foyer outside his therapist's office. I'd wondered what he'd look like and how he'd be dressed. But when I see him, there is only the essence of my big strapping son. We hug one another over and over, as if we haven't seen each other for a year—which is about true. Suddenly, just embracing Toren is the most joy I can imagine. It

147

doesn't seem possible that I'm kissing an addict, someone who would go through extreme pain and deception to get his drug of choice. I realize how much I love him and how much I desire him to live a productive and healthy life. The hugs are meant to enfold and protect him. But he's too full-grown. I know that Toren must do this for himself.

Another couple waits in the foyer as well, chatting with their loved one. They must be astounded by how happy I am. No one should be so joyful when greeting an addict. But I am. Toren's hair is damp and he explains that he'd just jumped out of the shower after playing touch football with a bunch of guys. Outdoors, a dusky autumn mist rises across the sweeping lawns. The levity of peace I feel, the knowledge I've gained today, and finally seeing my son in his new soberness, thrills me. Toren hanging on me with people watching, lets me know that he's happy, he's alive and fighting, alert, and looking for something better in his life. It's the exact moment I've been yearning for.

Toren and I spend over an hour with his therapist. Then we go to dinner at the cafeteria where we sit as long as possible and try to catch up on a year's worth of changes. The last time I saw him, he was walking away from us at the security gates of the airport heading to his assignment in the Peace Corps, neither of us dreaming our next meeting would be in a therapist's office at a rehab center for alcoholism. We separate that evening, knowing we will meet tomorrow with the entire family. Toren tells me how nervous he is to finally see his brothers.

When I return to the hotel that evening, I prepare the arriving family members for our seminar over the next two days. We watch an excellent documentary called, "The Hijacked Brain," about alcohol addiction, and discuss a packet of hand-outs I had collected that day. Together we compare our feelings about what has happened and mentally ready ourselves to meet Toren. We eat pizza and vegetables in our hotel room as we go over the materials. No one asks for a beer.

Our family's now due for a big vaccination. We know we need it and that it's good for us, but we don't know if we want to go there. I realize how anxious I am when we arrive in the parking lot the next morning. It's the same general location I'd parked the day before. I should recognize where I am. But it's a different space. I feel disoriented. "Where's the meeting being held?" my husband asks me.

"Over there," I tell him. Then I look at the agenda. "No, I mean, I think it's over *there*, in that bigger building." I point to the other side of the road and everyone looks the opposite direction.

"What do you mean? Don't you know?" he questions me. "Weren't you here yesterday?" Our sons sit quietly in the back seat like they did in grade school when their parents had disagreed. Waiting to see who would give in, what would happen. Uncomfortable.

Meetings the prior day had been in various locations throughout the campus. We'd climbed up and down the hill and been transported hither and thither in the official van. By now I don't know for sure where I should be at the moment. "Give me a break!" I look out the car windows hoping I will see something—a facade, a bush, a revealing sign—something to indicate where the hell we should be getting educated. I suddenly begin crying, holding my head in my hands above the steering wheel.

"Get a hold of yourself, Chris," my husband orders.

And I realize what a basket case I am. The saving moment occurs when I glimpse a participant from the prior day entering a building. "Over there!" I holler, thrilled to again be in control. But my sons are looking at me in dismay from the backseat. They hadn't realized how bad off I was. Now they know. I'm barely hanging together. (Weeks later I am able to email the brothers to tell them that I'm doing better. I explain that I'm now able to enter a parking lot and find my destination without having a nervous breakdown.)

When I'd first heard about Toren's alcoholism I was both horrified and relieved. Now we're here to "fix" it, and I know realistically that this weekend won't be enough. The reason I know this is because Toren himself called and said, "There's not an answer to this problem. That's what you're in rehab for, to find your own solution, one that works for you. You figure it out for yourself and get to work on it. No distractions allowed."

That's what our family has arranged for and what we're going to get. No distractions allowed. As the weekend unfolds, we spend hours with Toren and a few selected families, learning about how we will go through this together, about addiction and its impact on the family. Our boys express their love, looking at Toren as someone who is trapped but battling. And I see them dig in their heels to join up. Tears flow like a sprinkling fountain as we individually meet the disease and agree to do battle.

We hate the disease and detest what it has done to our family. But in its face, we unite so that it will not rob us of our *joie-de-vivre*. We stand up to it to declare that this disease will not destroy our family. Our Perfect Family. (Now, a somewhat humbler family.) *And* a family educated about alcoholism. We admit we've been jerked around by our own shortsightedness. And at the same time, we may thank this destructive disease for allowing us to pull together, to wake up to a progression of behaviors that could destroy others of us. Together we talk with Toren to create a plan for all of us, one that allows his success and encourages our involvement. This plan forces us to confront our own part of the equation, perhaps our enabling or co-dependency issues. We writhe as we think of what we need to do for our own lives.

On Saturday evening, Toren has a required activity at the rehab center, so we part and the four of us head out to a steakhouse for dinner. Another dagger hits home when I realize we are dining on red meat (in the type of place that serves those exploding batter-fried onions) and we're *not* drinking alcohol. Our sons are in their mid twenties and if it had been a normal dinner out on a Saturday night, we would've probably ordered a beer or a glass of wine.

As we sip our lemonades and cokes during the meal, we can't help but go over all that has transformed us. We laugh; we talk about the boys' lives. They're in transitional phases and we seldom have the luxury of meeting together without other people or intrusions. It's just us talking. The evening takes on a philosophical bent with a dash of science; several of our family members pursue healthcare careers and discuss the rehab program from their perspective. Critiques are made in good spirit. We realize that there are those who question the spiritual nature of the 12-Step Program, its definition of addiction as an incurable disease and the long-term dependence on the program.[56]

Certainly, other approaches to the treatment of alcoholism exist. There is more than one choice for an active, diligent program of recovery and some programs may be well suited to one person but not to another. But presently more than 93 percent of U.S. treatment centers utilize the AA approach.[57] Toren has selected a regime oriented to the Twelve Steps, and we are here to encourage him and to stand with him. We're on a learning curve and even with questions, we honor all that we've experienced and heard because we wish for Toren's healing and growth. And we love him.

By the end of the weekend on Sunday afternoon, we've met some of Toren's new friends, his favorite priest, his therapist, and countless others who help us map our journey as a recovering family. This baptism into alcoholism has transformed our Perfect Family dynamics, as Toren had predicted. Now we are armed with better knowledge about alcohol addiction; we have taken the opportunity to ask Toren about his disease; we have told Toren how the disease has affected us; we have worked out specific strategies to help Toren within our family; we have promised to support one another and Toren in his recovery.

At our final lunch with Toren, we find out even more about his demise over the past two years. For spontaneous recreation, the brothers have a few moments to elbow one another and chase around the parking lot (as they have always done in every existing parking lot for no particular reason). It convinces me that things could get back to "normal."

Then we say good-bye to him. Toren has nine more days of rehab to complete, and we must return to our lives in other parts of the U.S. Our farewell hugs are strong and fortifying. We know that all of us have changed. Visiting hours have terminated.

19

SHATTERING MY WILL

All in all, I was in rehab for 33 days. Before checking out of my D.C. hotel and checking into rehab, my assessment counselor, Carl, told me that I probably wouldn't get to return to service. I said okay, I guess, but asked that they please keep an open mind to the idea and not fully close the door on it because I knew that I'd be able to handle going back. He told me that after my time was up in rehab, I might not feel ready to return back to South America. Sure, whatever.

The staff in rehab stressed that they were trying to squeeze a year's worth of education and information into one month's time through lectures, seminars, one-on-one and group therapy and other activities. With a big cheesy smile, a counselor always repeated the same thing to us, "Oh, no, don't worry people, there's only one thing we plan to change about you here, and that one thing is everything." Ha, ha. Fuck off.

Eventually, toward the end of my stay in rehab, I was able to say, "Hi, my name is Toren, and I'm an alcoholic." With time, I slowly began to realize what it all meant. I had to take apart and undo much of my thinking, re-examine my attitudes and confront things that had always seemed normal to me in my social settings. Some attitudes conducive to my drinking no longer worked for me. I had to learn that alcoholism was not only a disease, but that I had it. I wrote this passage in my journal early on, but didn't really believe it until weeks later:

*These (older) patients are not acting. They are fighting everyday and they were **YOU** once. You need to listen to them.*

*You are here for a reason and **HAVE** time to choose your path.*
***THIS** will destroy you if you don't believe that you could be*
*them and that you have this. This **DISEASE** will ruin you and take*
everything you love and that loves you. Listen and be glad.

My circumstances seemed so much better than many other
people's. I was still young, had less physical and emotional damage,
and I had no pending legal issues by comparison. More importantly,
I had escaped without devastating a family or any person I loved
and had not attempted to kill anyone or myself. It is hard when
you are good at looking past and minimizing your own issues,
especially when you are living in rehab where almost everyone is
as screwed up, or much more so, than you.

In that case, the forever kicking disease in me says that I'm
not so bad. I am okay and this is all an over-reaction. *That* hasn't
happened to me. YET. It is easy to see all the fun I had and listen to
other people's stories and start to tell myself that I'm really all
right and I certainly haven't hit bottom. Somewhere in *The Big Book*
(the AA book), a writer says, "You hit bottom when you stop
digging."

If I am anything like other alcoholics—and I am—my path is
leading to the same place almost all untreated alcoholics end up:
to jails, institutions, or death. I had the opportunity to be what
they call here in the world of recovery a "high-bottom drunk."
What I was quickly made aware of by my counselor is that, in my
mind, I tended to glorify drinking and completely minimize how
serious it had gotten for me. It has always been part of my nature
to shrug off the bad, find the good, and move on. I was told that in
this case I needed to focus on what was going wrong for me in
the last few years and to examine the trail of legal and behavioral
problems that I had left behind. Ooohh, yeeeahh, that.

To me, the good times easily outnumbered the bad ten-fold. But
scattered problems consistently checkered my past. Unlike an athlete
or performer who may easily see and remember past mistakes, my
alcoholism taught me to recognize only the pleasure. I completely
erased all the unpleasant consequences as soon as possible, whereas
someone 'normal' may have quit or been scared straight.

Part of alcohol addiction is the insanity surrounding the disease, shared by the alcoholic and the family or loved ones around them. There is an irrational conviction that things are going to get better, change, or that the problem will go away. And after doing the same thing over and over again—drinking—I was consistently getting a similar result over and over again, one that was quickly worsening. What had been cumulatively tolerable was beginning to add up and eat away at me. Lying in bed at night sweating or twitching and fearing seizures eventually broke down my stubborn alcoholic defenses. I knew I was screwed-up but it took a lot for me to believe it, want to confront it, and go to anyone about it. (Asking for help is for sissies, right?) But I had lost control.

One of the biggest parts of the process, and a foundation of the Twelve Steps, is admitting powerlessness. If you can't accept that you are powerless, there is a good chance that you will have to go another round or two with whatever was kicking your ass all the way to rehab.

Powerlessness was a tough one for me, like most alcoholics who think they are in control and delude themselves into believing it through distorted perceptions and sick thinking. I had to come to terms with the fact that, once I started drinking, I was exercising less and less control every time I drank and I was beginning to behave just like any normal addict in pursuit of his substance. It was terrible. *Not me.*

During one of our evening meetings in rehab, we were asked to share our thoughts and feelings on powerlessness and how it relates to our use and recovery. Suddenly it occurred to me that I had the perfect little anecdote to share about my powerlessness.

I told them how my will had been completely shattered through the All-Volunteer Conference and how I became aware of it as it happened. I went from thinking I would just drink a little the first night, to blacking out the second night, and then later on in the week, having to scurry to the store midway during lectures to get liquor in order to prevent detox. I had become totally powerless and was beginning to realize it for the first time.

There was more that happened when I went on my little trip to get liquor. More interestingly, the incident with the buggy seems to capture the progression of my loss of control.

Flashback...On my way to the liquor store, walking through the up-scale residential area (when I should have been attending the project workshop), the horse and buggy that I came across was actually unattended. I thought to myself, "What would I do if I were me?" I decided I would not impulsively jump in, that I'd wait to see if the buggy remained there when I returned. How rational and responsible. Then I purchased my liquor so I could cure myself.

Now, here is what *really* happened with the horse and buggy. As I reapproached the still-unattended rig for the second time, yet to open my drink, I concluded that this *is* the kind of thing I would do. And besides, I was down in South America to experience new things, and this presented a crazy chance to live in the moment and go for it.

I gave an innocent look around and saw no one. Trying to act as normal as possible, I climbed into the square-shaped wooden cart-like vehicle. There were two black horses attached to the reins I now held. I lit up, trying to hide my smile, and adrenaline rushed in.

What the hell was I doing? I gave them a whip and a feeble, "Heeyaah." Nothing happened.

This time with some excitement, "HeeeyaaaAAAAHHH!!!" Again, there was no response.

I stood up, laughing at myself, wondering what I had to do get these bastards to get a move on. I gave 'em a good tug, followed by a whip and an assertive, "*Jaha!!*" (Let's go!) and we jerked forward.

We were finally moving and I was elated. I passed a pedestrian on the fairly wide neighborhood road, smiling, trying to cover up any mischief that may have been showing on my face. Cracking the whip two more times, I moved our trot up to a more satisfying pace. We proceeded along pretty well when we suddenly veered left at a 45-degree angle onto another street. This hadn't been my command. We now headed in a direction that wouldn't get me any closer to where I wanted to go—our volunteer workshop.

Since there was no one around, I gave another crack of the whip and a shout. I was good! After the initial excitement wore off, I thought about slowing down. On the left an oncoming car passed me and I began thinking that I should end my joyride. I tried to get the horses to decelerate with a few inventive pulls and jerks, like I'd learned riding horseback, but they ignored any of my commands. We raced pretty fast. I pondered a Hollywood bailout over the side then I reconsidered.

Up a block, I noticed a parked car that seemed to zip towards us. I tried again to slow the horses, to steer, but we were hauling ass and they had their own agenda. If the horses were trying to dash away from me it wasn't going to work because they were pulling me right along behind them. I started getting freaked out. 'Oh shit, oh shit,' I thought to myself, 'These guys have to know what they're doing.' I sure didn't. The parked car 'sped' directly at us and we were aligned to clip its whole left side. It now occurred to me that these horses weren't worried about anything; they seemed to be sprinting out of fright. Whoops. 'No way, no way, no way in hell! This isn't happening!' ran through my mind.

I wanted to jump out, freeze the situation. Or start the ride over. But it was way too late and certainly out of my hands. Suddenly, we nailed the car. We hit the left front part of the bumper, scraping along its side. My weather-beaten cart then slowed down just enough for me to leap out while the crazed horses madly thundered on down the street, leaving me with my disaster in complete disbelief. Incredibly, there was still no one around. Petrified and shocked, I felt damn stupid. Guilty.

What the hell was that? The problem I'd caused was overwhelming and I was at a loss how to fix it. So, like any good foreign ambassador of the U.S. Government, I ran like hell. Thank goodness, in the end, everything was okay. For me.

This could-be exhilarating experience quickly turned horrifying. But experiencing this humiliation still wasn't enough to stop me from drinking. In fact, it was even more reason to drink: to calm the old nerves and reflect on what a crazy mishap I had just created.

With further reflection, this significant moment embodied a lot of my experiences with alcohol. It started with experimentation, moved to a bad decision or two, then excitement and adventure progressed into an episode of problems, consequences, and eventual loss of direction and control.

In rehab, I was able to learn and eventually start to accept the ugliness of the disease of alcoholism and how it was beginning to take shape for me. Experience shows that alcoholism is a chronic and progressive disease. Going back out and trying to control drinking again will only give me worse results.

20

WHAT TO TELL GRANDMA

OCTOBER 2003. THEY COME AROUND IN THE MOST INNOCENT WAY and ask a question that knocks you flat. "How's Toren doing in South America?" or "What've you heard from Toren lately?" You can't escape friends and family.

It's hard not to be honest. We remind Toren during his rehab program that people are constantly inquiring about him and we don't know what to say when they ask. It's been three weeks now that we've been avoiding their inquiries. And then, at the Family Education Weekend, Toren says to us, "Go ahead, tell 'em. Tell anyone. I want everyone to know." It's a relief to hear that. Now I can inform the people who care. Now I can get the support we need. Now I can be honest.

Toren wants to phone his closest friends upon his release from rehab. All the family agrees to wait until he's had a chance to do this before we tell any of them. It seems like this should be a private thing. But alcoholism is not secret. It reeks. And all those around must know, especially if they are to support the alcoholic's recovery.

I am able to tell my best friends about Toren as soon as I return home from the Family Education Weekend. These confidantes are women who have stood by my side throughout the years, who harbor my hopes and fears, who have cried and laughed with me. I practice my story in my mind. Then I invite two of them to my home, pour tea and coffee, and make a fire. We sit down and they know I am about to explode with some sort of terrible news. They've watched me avoid my life for the past three weeks, lose weight, not return their phone calls, and they know I recently disappeared for a weekend for no reason. I practice my story. Then burst into tears when I tell them—finally.

It has been too long keeping this angst to myself. Surprisingly, they listen then express their happiness that Toren has come forward on his own, that he has decided to take care of this for himself. The judgment I'd feared is absent. In its place is empathy and understanding. As I begin to learn, almost everyone has an alcoholic in the family background and countless people have endured the dysfunction of this disease. My friends line up beside me to fortify our family; they write letters to our son expressing confidence in his recovery. I feel a burden taken off my shoulders as they grab on. During the next week, I spend time calling several of our closest friends, especially those who have supported Toren throughout the years.

Each time I see someone in the community, I wonder if I should explain what we have faced the last two months. When they ask about Toren, I have to decide if they are ready to hear about him and whether they really care. Some of them are mothers of his classmates. Knowing what I do now, I think, "Whose kid is next?"

Don works each day with numerous nurses and surgeons in the operating room. Conversations about children and what they're doing are common, especially when a case drags on for hours. There are some medical personnel whom Don feels comfortable telling about Toren. But on the periphery, there are those who are asking about his family in the same way one would say, "How're you today?" Don decides to tell his closest associates as the occasion presents. With each disclosure, he is comforted by those who have faced similar obstacles. And by those who fear similar problems with their own adolescents.

Family Education at the rehab center gives us realistic hope for Toren's future and a spot for each of us in his recovery. But it also offers a terse warning about relapse.[58] We are told that relapse rates for addictive diseases range from 50 percent (for resumption of heavy use) to 90 percent (for a brief relapse). "Relapse should not be viewed as a failure; it is part of a learning process that eventually leads to recovery," says Susan Gordon of the Caron Foundation.[59]

I realize that it's important to let our extended family know about Toren as soon as possible so that they can aid Toren in being honest about himself and his goals. There remain grandparents and aunts and uncles to be informed. These visits and phone calls seem even more ominous to me than meeting with our friends. I steel myself to make the plunge. At the same time as I prepare to contact our family members, newly-humbled Rush Limbaugh has just returned to his radio show after five weeks of rehab for addiction to pain killers. "This is not something someone can do alone," he admits in USA Today.[60] Limbaugh has twenty million fans (and perhaps a grandma) to support him, even though he has previously blasted drug abuse saying users should be jailed.

Toren could face strict judgment from those relatives who march the moral high road. These are people who see only one path for spiritual belief and maintain that Toren (and all of our family) could better solve our problems by joining their particular faith. We all dread facing these people. When measured by their standards, of course we fall short. Don and I and our boys have talked together about how we will deal with this. Oddly, when faith should be so forgiving, so compassionate, we feel our hearts flutter and our stomach acids boil as we anticipate approaching these enlightened, happily-religious persons. But they are family. We know they love us and we have to deal with their versions of spirituality.

I begin with Grandma, our most vociferous relative. Here I am, approaching a family of virgin drinkers; there has never been an alcoholic in this family tree. We're torquing the first branch. To ease into it, I play a game of racquetball with my father, and then take him and my mother to lunch. At this time, I tell them what has happened: that Toren is now back in the U.S.; how he committed himself to a rehab program; how our family attended the Family Education Program; and how proud we are of Toren's courage and fortitude. I talk about the disease of alcoholism, give them the Jellinek Curve and some articles about the brain and the effects of dopamine and addiction. I explain to them ways they can support our family.

Both grandparents seem understanding, though crushed. They are so shocked that they don't react much. But I fear there will be *those* comments.

The next day I receive a call from one son saying he just talked with Grandma who asked him why he and his brothers drink but not his girl cousins. She also remarked that had Toren been reading his Bible, he could have saved himself. Our son is upset and doesn't want to tell Grandma she has insulted our family. He wants our family to be unified, but I hear the discouragement in his voice.

The next day, I print out a large index card for my parents and leave it on their kitchen counter beside the phone. I hope that seeing the written words will reinforce some of the ideas we had talked about the previous day. The red ink suggests:

Ways to Help the Recovery of Our Family

✓ Talk about <u>today</u> and our goals for today and how you support Toren (and us) NOW.
  Do not talk about past behaviors you've noticed.
  Do not say, "I saw this coming."

✓ Talk about how you support your grandkids NOW.
  Do not compare grandkids and their behaviors—you do not really know about their true behaviors.

✓ Allow each person to have his/her own faith.
  Do not interject how you think faith should be. Do not bring up faith. Leave our faith to us, please.

✓ If you don't know what to say, try this:
  "I love you and admire your courage. How can I support you?" And then say no more.

✓ Attend Al-Anon

After leaving the prompts for Grandma, things go better. My father confides to me several weeks later how proud he is of the way Don and I are handling it all. Both of my parents attend Al-Anon with me once a week. We begin our recovery as a stumbling bunch of neophytes.

And then the aunts and uncles in our family step up. One uncle, a minister and college professor, volunteers to meet Toren at his rehab graduation and drive him back to Washington, D.C., for his exit interview. Other family members clamor to visit him but it is impossible because they live too far away and his rehab is almost completed. I spend hours talking with each relative about the things we've learned and our family's commitment to face our disease. It's a relief to confess what we've discovered, to realize that people will accept us. Toren calls me after we arrive back home from our weekend education and comments, "I've received a lot of mail and cards. I must be really popular or really sick."

The *Truth* is, religion or no religion, our family came through in a big way. The relatives were helpful and loving and supported us beyond our wildest hopes. Our fears of judgment were, for the most part, unfounded. Perhaps this, too, is a lesson that Toren forced upon our family. It caused us to let down some of our spiritual barriers, to realize that no matter what a person believes, we are all in this together, and that the family gathers around when an individual is in need.

The first step of the Twelve Steps is admitting our powerlessness over alcohol—that our lives had become unmanageable. I realize that this step not only applies to the alcoholic, but to his family. By letting go of the control, I am learning the language of recovery. I see how it covers various aspects of my life, not just the specific disease of alcoholism. When I am able to give up controlling the image of my family and be truthful about our challenge, I become empowered by the focus of my friends and family who move towards us. We are offered understanding, compassion, and wisdom.

A helpful set of ideas was given to us at our education weekend. I keep it tucked inside my wallet; whenever I open it to complete a transaction, I review the following principles:

Let Go

✓ To let go does not mean to stop caring, it means I can't do it for someone else.

✓ To let go is not to cut myself off, it's the realization I can't control another.

✓ To let go is not to enable, but to allow learning from natural consequences.

✓ To let go is to admit powerlessness, which means the outcome is not in my hands.

✓ To let go is not to try to change or blame another, it's to make the most of myself.

✓ To let go is not to care for, but to care about.

✓ To let go is not to fix, but to be supportive.

✓ To let go is not to judge, but to allow another to be a human being.

✓ To let go is not to be in the middle arranging all the outcomes but to allow others to affect their own destinies.

✓ To let go is not to be protective, it's to permit another to face reality.

✓ To let go is not to deny, but to accept.

✓ To let go is not to nag, scold or argue, but instead, to search out my own shortcomings and to correct them.

✓ To let go is not to adjust everything to my desires but to take each day as it comes, and to cherish myself in it.

✓ To let go is not to criticize and regulate anybody but to try to become what I dream I can be.

✓ To let go is not to regret the past, but to grow and live for the future.

✓ To let go is to fear less and to love more.[61]

We talk with Toren's brothers about looking at a new way of socializing within our family. Without alcohol. One brother says, "Our brother's no different to us. We will still throw the football around and goof off. We've gone most of our lives without alcohol and it won't change for us. If someone else can't do that, then they don't have to be with us." I smile and realize that, afterall, we weren't constantly guzzling alcohol in the household. It seems that the last few weeks it was all I could think about. As if it were served at every meal. It wasn't.

While our own family seems comfortable with the concessions of alcoholism, the brothers' level of socializing with buddies will be a greater adjustment. They admit that they've relied on alcohol to fuel their fun when they're among friends. One brother says, "I have no problem with not drinking. But it'll be weird with our friends because we've done it for so many years. And we have the same friends." The boys are now thinking about this. When the time comes, when one day Toren returns home, then they can discuss it and deal with it. For now, I see the value of a halfway situation. It will allow Toren time to develop social tools so that he can navigate outside his safety zone.

Don and I laugh as we realize we've now gone forty days and forty nights without drinking! If Grandma knew, she would fall to her artificial knees in gratitude. It seems like our family's getting smarter about alcoholism. Toren has offered us this chance, even when we wanted to push it away. With this, I understand that wisdom is what you know when it's already too late.

21

HALFWAY HOME

30 October 2003. So great then, I completed my rehab. Everything's cool, right? Now send me back to South America. I still have unfinished business and a lot of work to do. But unfortunately, I have more work to do here than in South America.

Whether I could or could not return to service, and complete it successfully with what I now know, is unimportant. It is obvious that I should not go back right now. I learned that I need to stop making all of the decisions and be open to suggestion, be willing to ask for help and stay close to The Program.

What the hell am I supposed to do? Living in a halfway house sounds pretty good for a start, right? Sure, I'll go from a functioning volunteer living on my own in South America, to a soothing transition from an inpatient rehab program, to living quarters that suggest I am not yet capable of functioning on my own. Hey, after a month, my curfew gets an hour later! I can already taste the freedom.

The biggest thing I need to do is come to terms with my disease. This means consistently accepting it and understanding what it means to say that I am powerless over alcohol. Yeah, yeah, I'm sure anyone can argue the semantics of powerlessness and what it means to surrender. I was a pretty firm believer that I wasn't addicted to alcohol and that I had control over it. Maybe there is some truth to it, or maybe not.

But I am learning about alcoholism. And I have learned that I am an alcoholic. This means that when I start drinking, it becomes increasingly difficult to stop or control the amount of drinks I put into myself. To anyone, this should sound just like a heroin addict, right? Always at risk of overdosing. It is. Once clean, no one tells a heroin addict or a cokehead to just shoot-up with moderation, on weekends, or after work. Or just do one or two lines. No one tells a former chain smoker, after having quit for a year, to have a social smoke on occasion. Alcohol isn't any different for the alcoholic.

The connection of alcohol being as dangerous to an alcoholic as heroin to a heroin addict isn't often made, partially because business booms around alcohol. Alcohol is still a drug and some people don't process it normally. Just like heroin, the tolerance raises. Addicts increasingly do more and more heroin because they require it and they will do anything to get it. In the end, they lose control. With alcohol it tends to be a slower process and it is more socially acceptable.

Because this process happened pretty fast for me, I discovered I was an alcoholic fairly early. It isn't always noticed by age twenty-three. If one isn't an alcoholic, there is no reason to say, "Okay, self, I'm only going to have three drinks this time." Normal people don't sit around and think up plans for how much they are going to not drink every night. They do whatever feels right and it doesn't progressively go downhill. If you think you have a problem with drinking, you probably do. According to most alcoholics, 'drinking problems' don't get better or go away and, with time, any uncertainty usually gives way to only more concrete signs.

There are lots of misunderstandings about 12-Step Programs, and that is fine because if you don't understand them or haven't found yourself in a position to be exposed to them, congratulations, you may not ever need them. The thing that struck me most about the 12-Step Program was that it's really just a simple plan for living. You may hear about people who are constantly working the Steps or that they follow a tight program or you may not. Again, congratulations.

The 12-Step Program is not a system where one graduates from one step to the next and then moves on, never working the previous one again. The Steps require constant acknowledgement of powerlessness, acceptance, reliance on sources of help outside one's self, admitting one's faults and correcting wrongs as well as helping others. These aspects, constantly being worked, allow one to concentrate on oneself from the inside-out, to eventually heal spiritually, and to repair damaged relationships in one's life. It is actually surprisingly in-line with a lot of the fundamentals of mainstream organized religion, while focusing on staying open to individual interpretation. The 12-Step Program is relevant to any faith, and all persons are able to pray to a God of their understanding or a Higher Power to help them do what they couldn't do for themselves. It could be considered more of an all-denominational rather than a non-denominational fellowship.

I freaked out during my first days in rehab because of how many times I heard God mentioned in the Steps, in prayers, and in the program's reliance on His powers to take away our character defects, as well as our obsessions and compulsions to drink. Healing an addict is something that is considered to be impossible through human power alone. I wrote a shit-load in my journal, scrambling, trying to find a working definition of my Higher Power. I was not going to spend a month in rehab and have to wince or fake it every time I heard or said the word 'God.' To say the least, I have always had strong feelings about certain parts of organized religions and have hated feeling pressure to 'be something' whether it be Christian, Muslim, Jewish or, I guess, Alcoholic. Besides, our family has seen some pretty drastic divisions due to religious differences. How was this deity dividing our family rather than uniting it? What would this 'God' do for me in rehab?

As mentioned earlier, for my Higher Power, I decided to rely on my family, friends, music, nature in all its perfection and imperfection, to be my sources of strength. I figured that would cover it. Some theologians would probably say that God manifests Himself in all of those things. Well, great, then we're all happy. I learned that, rather than jump right to God, we could turn to the program for help and use the people in the fellowship as a source of guidance and strength. This made it a little bit easier on me. I didn't have to fake it.

One of the more influential chaplains at rehab once said that if you are searching for God, then you have already found Him. When speaking to one of my uncles, a minister and Bible teacher, about some of my issues and questions about recovery and the search for God, he asked, "Well, can you imagine what it would be like if your search *did* end, and you *did* find what you were looking for?" Whoa...good point. New subject.

There. I'm fixed.

I know I'm an alcoholic. I have my 12-Step Program, ten thousand versions of God to choose from, and I know that as long as I don't drink then I won't suffer anymore, right? Maybe. But what about all the fun everyone else is still having? Why did that same bastard Higher Power make me a drunk?

This Higher Power that is so merciful and is going to bail me out of all these crazy problems had to make me different in the first place, huh? Maybe it isn't so great after all. Saving me, my ass. Now I can't do what most people do throughout their twenties and thirties, or even their whole lives: drink and socialize without problems.

"Now, Toren, everything happens for a reason."

Shut up. Ok, I may be sobering up, but that doesn't entirely fix the problem. I know that asking for help and being honest with myself probably made things a lot easier on me. Instead of trying to be an apple among oranges, while totally suffering and trying to control my drinking, I can start to deal with this and move on.

"It's going to make you stronger as a person."

Shut up. I know that leaving South America and being in rehab was what I needed, not what I wanted. Now I'm a graduate from rehab and I get to live in a halfway house. Now I'm officially an Alcoholic. Damn. Now I'm another statistic, newly categorized, and all those wonderful stigmas can follow me and be attached to my family, as well.

Now everyone can worry about my sobriety, not my drinking. Now everyone can be self-conscious about drinking around me, thinking about drinking around me, or just joking about drinking. Now the seed has been firmly planted in my head and I can never go back and think of drinking normally again. Do I sound happy? Who cares? I'll get over it. I've already cried a river and things could be *a lot* worse. It pisses me off but there is a lot of life to live and I know it wasn't working the way I was doing it.

So there has to be a brighter side somewhere to suffocating my social life and not having fun anymore.

"Lighten up, sobriety is great."

I guess what is more important is that I need to comprehend that it's not the world's responsibility to understand my problem. There certainly won't be a 'holiday-on-Fridays-extending-the-weekend' for the rest of the partiers because Toren quit drinking. I guess then, I have to get over myself, and maybe stop writing like anyone else cares.

What's that? Someone asked what might have been done to prevent this from happening. Ban alcohol. Whoops. Prohibit all alcoholics from reproducing, maybe? Now that's an idea. I bet my Higher Power is smiling now. If we eliminated addicts and alcoholics then we wouldn't need any Higher Powers, right?

I guess what I wasn't trying to say, but mean to say, is that alcoholism is not easy to prevent. Young kids or teenagers are not apt to cooperate. They'll meet restrictions with resistance. I sure as hell didn't want to comply and I still have trouble taking back all my questionable decisions and defiance. They were good times that I shall no longer glorify. OOOOWWW!!

It is said that the older the habit, the harder it is to break. It looks like it's tough to prevent alcoholism at any age or from any direction. I think the key to this is having the desire to stop—something I hope I actually have and can stay in touch with. As far as preventing it from even starting, good luck with that. People need to learn from their own experiences and this often needs to run its course. For example, when climbing a mountain, how many would stop before reaching their desired destination if on their way down, a couple people say, "It's not worth it." People need to see it to believe it. Well, I did anyway.

Looking back, it may seem obvious that I had a problem from the beginning. One of the biggest questions may be whether intervention would have been a good idea and, if so, when? I think it should be emphasized again that most people in the early stages of addiction are in denial (at best) and usually extremely stubborn about any idea of change. Before great losses or consequences surface, the path to powerlessness is well underway. Authorities, concerned family members or friends may recognize warning signs before the actual abuser admits to having a problem. If intervention is used, the type of intervention and how it would be implemented should be carefully strategized. Some chronic drinkers may be more receptive than I would have been. Normally, the impetus for change begins further along, when the abuser is ready to seek help.

It is easy to keep second guessing the seriousness of an alcohol crisis. No one wants a real problem to exist. Each alcoholic's symptoms manifest in different ways, and some may present themselves more slowly than others. Certain alcoholics may get into trouble with the law, while others find themselves acting out and treating people completely different while intoxicated. Others may have control issues or black out from time to time. Many alcoholics may not experience much difficulty in the beginning, which makes comparisons among addicts misleading. There is plenty of room to rationalize and redefine the idea of an alcohol problem when being forced to look closely at oneself or having to actually change behaviors. It often becomes difficult to say who really has a problem until it is too late.

The power of denial is stronger than one would think. In May of 2002, I drove up the coast of California with a good friend of mine named Chad. He opened up a direct line by speaking about his own drinking problems to me. But I still wasn't ready for it. I wasn't able to understand it or see its relation to me.

Chad explained to me how he *knew* he was an alcoholic and had been going to AA meetings. I was kind of surprised. He told me that he *knew* he was powerless over alcohol; he could not stop drinking when he started and he almost invariably lost control of his intoxication and, consequently, a lot of his actions. I tried to console him, without daring to mention that I felt I had my own problems with alcohol.

There I was, staring my own disease in the face. I was so unwilling to admit my own problems that I didn't even want to accept that he had a problem. *Us—have a problem?* I told him he should limit how much he drinks. "Just don't drink so much, dude; you're all right." I didn't believe him when he said he couldn't stop drinking or that he was losing control.

It took me another year (and then some) to begin to understand this...the hard way. After further research in the field of binge drinking, Chad and I entered different rehabs the same month without contacting each other or knowing that the other had finally given up.

How many other people could be reading this and not be willing to look at their own problems with alcohol? My guess is a lot. I know I could have. Alcoholism may hide behind its numerous faces and with its variety of symptoms, but they worsen and don't go away. For this same reason, both Chad and I 'threw in the towel.' Many others may find that the fight is not worth it anymore and that there is hope. It seems to require a different path for each person to discover an understanding of this twisted disease, and how it may or may not personally apply.

My perception of reality had been slowly altering for so long that almost anything was endurable as long as I knew I could do what I wanted. It never occurred to me until way too late, I didn't have to go through all the abuse. It is no different than any unhealthy or exploitive relationship, perhaps similar to someone with a serious eating disorder. Normal is abnormal, and unsafe becomes safe. Someone in an abusive relationship becomes accustomed to this type of treatment, stops questioning it, and even begins to think that she deserves it or that it is her own fault. Much of this was true in my case. All of my negative consequences were the result of my 'choosing' to drink, and when things got even worse, I began to accept things as normal that were actually self-destructive.

I was willing to do whatever it took to continue drinking the way I wanted, whether it was high school or college. I knew it was extreme but never thought I was 'sick' or that my behavior was inappropriate. I blended in with others who drank heavily and that made it difficult for me to be identified as alcoholic. Punishments and threats just caused avoidance, created more secretive behaviors and, at best, short term compliance. Grounding me, kicking me off sports teams, taking away social privileges or my car, putting me in jail, making me pay fines, all this did little or nothing for me.

Intervention at that point in my drinking would never have worked because the majority of my drinking was social, in a party atmosphere, and without regret. Only when I was flung to the other side of the spectrum, where I was met with seriously adverse physical symptoms, did I even come close to considering an alternative. By this time, it was far too late and all the red-flag behavioral issues that could ideally have been prevented were said and done. I could have been shipped off to rehab in high school or maybe college, but it would not have changed my mentality. The classic 'at least we tried' may have comforted some, but in the end, I had to come to terms with drinking on my own.

There are some factors that influenced my alcohol awareness in a positive way. Many were subtle and finally may have added up; some weighed more heavily than others as I wove my way in and out of trouble. To assist a person in danger (in place of using intervention), there may be understated approaches for offering:

- ✓ Persistent emotional support
- ✓ Continual reminders and warnings of red flags
- ✓ Education about alcohol
- ✓ Open dialogue on the possible outcomes of alcoholism and addiction

For example, learning in my initial AA meetings (the ones required by my college RD) that frequent blackouts don't happen to normal drinkers and that I was at risk for alcoholism, helped me first become aware. Through experiencing unusual hangovers, anxiety, fevers and sweating, and continually feeling more threatened by the possibility of seizures, I began to live the early stages of alcoholism. These ugly realities were what it took to bring about change.

Similar to the onset of all alcoholism, change is something that will not happen overnight and no one recovers unless they want to. Until a person is ready to sober up, he will fight it with everything he has.

Knowing that alcoholism is a disease, is passed on through heredity and is prevalent in my family, helps me to understand my situation more today. More than that, knowing that alcoholism is a livable disease makes me feel fortunate. The real aspect of this disease is that there is plenty of hope for the hopeless; all they have to do is want help. The 12-Step Programs can literally save anybody from that point on.

Recognizing my problem and becoming aware of its consequences has assisted me significantly. I was educated about alcohol; all the warning signs had been pointed out to me. Credit is due to my parents and some counselors at college who made me look at myself. (None of this stopped my behavior but it made me aware.)

Since turning myself in, I have found the most advantageous strategy for the present is:

✓ To shut up.

✓ To listen to people with experience.

✓ To realize that 'my way' didn't and won't work.

✓ To continue asking for help.

✓ To stay honest with myself.

✓ To keep an openness and willingness to do what is necessary.

It has also been crucial to have a supportive family that, rather than pointing fingers, shows unconditional love. It helps to know we are powerless over other people, powerless over certain substances, and powerless over many events going on around us.

And on top of everything, honesty is fundamental. If you're honest with yourself, you're halfway there.

22

MOVING ON TO GRAVY

GRAVY

NO OTHER WORD WILL DO. FOR THAT'S WHAT IT WAS. GRAVY.
GRAVY, THESE PAST TEN YEARS.
ALIVE, SOBER, WORKING, LOVING AND
BEING LOVED BY A GOOD WOMAN. ELEVEN YEARS
AGO HE WAS TOLD HE HAD SIX MONTHS TO LIVE
AT THE RATE HE WAS GOING. AND HE CHANGED HIS WAYS
SOMEHOW. HE QUIT DRINKING! AND THE REST?
AFTER THAT IT WAS *ALL* GRAVY, EVERY MINUTE
OF IT, UP TO AND INCLUDING WHEN HE WAS TOLD ABOUT,
WELL, SOME THINGS THAT WERE BREAKING DOWN AND
BUILDING UP INSIDE HIS HEAD. "DON'T WEEP FOR ME,"
HE SAID TO HIS FRIENDS. "I'M A LUCKY MAN.
I'VE HAD TEN YEARS LONGER THAN I OR ANYONE
EXPECTED. PURE GRAVY. AND DON'T FORGET IT."

RAYMOND CARVER, *ALL OF US* [62]

DECEMBER 2003. THE DISEASE OF ALCOHOLISM IS STILL SNEAKING AROUND. Perhaps I've long-known what *Our Drink* would be about. Could be that's why I had those nights of tossing and turning. I just don't know what the last chapter will say. *There is no last chapter.*

The real word about drinking isn't out yet. It hasn't hit the cul-de-sac. The end of the road, a niche where you can turn around if you want to, is perceived to be a safe place to raise your Perfect Family. But in reality, this is a semi-circle where we parents tremble in fear as we collect the morning paper, dreading to find our passed-out teenager wallowing in a flowerbed since 2 a.m. the morning prior. Or discovering our kid parked in the driveway blacked-out since 3 a.m., slumped inside the car with windows up and motor still running. Things like that ruin the newspaper article we were about to read late morning over a tepid cup of coffee.

Even when a parent thinks she's aware of creeping alcoholism in her family, there comes a definite moment of lucidity. The first day I went to Family Education at the rehab facility, I remember sitting down by a matronly woman in a purple shirt. I chose to sit by her on purpose because I was scared and humiliated to be there. Somehow I thought the purple color of her clothing would comfort me. The stark chairs in the meeting room felt uncomfortable even while the purple woman smiled at me. So I forced myself to look squarely at her nametag. Her first name only, of course. And we whispered our introductions. She beamed sweetly as she explained, "This's my second program. My son relapsed last week." Then, as if to reassure me, she added, "But the other program was on the west coast. We decided to try this one."

I thought I would become ill. It seemed incomprehensible that someone would go through a program like this even *once*. But twice? How could it be? I looked her over more carefully. There must be a reason she would have a relapsed son. My son certainly wouldn't do *that*. But she was no slob; her color-coordinated outfit matched her corduroy pants; she was well-groomed and she looked calm. Not even bored, though we hadn't begun the session yet. There I sat on an inhospitable chair, emotionally frozen, and speechless as I realized that maybe *perhaps* just *somehow*, not only would I be completing this program one time, but *two* times. Or three. What was this disease of alcoholism, anyway? Did it have no sense of when to stop?

Ultimately, the purple woman and I both graduated from Family Weekend. I don't know how she and her relapsed son are doing. Well, I hope. But as our son begins his halfway program, I wonder what he will do in real life, whether or not I will be forced to wear a purple shirt. What about when he returns home to Olympia, a site where he "used"—*It's the water!* The motto and the town's name are synonymous, just like the American image of alcohol as a benign legal beverage. (The news, coincidentally about the same time as Toren finishes rehab, is that the former brewery in our town is presently being purchased by a water bottling company. Is that a good omen? The dark side of me is laughing hysterically. Now my sons can meet their friends at the brewery for water-making tours!)

When the boys were small, they helped me with the yard work. One job was weeding. In the Northwest, cedar and fir trees volunteer all over the place between tulips and under rhododendrons. The boys hated pulling them out, knowing the tiny trees were destined for certain death, so I allowed them to transplant the seedlings to a backdoor section of earth alongside our house. They dubbed it their "tree farm" and spent hours stabbing tiny sprigs of cedar and Douglas fir into the soil. Years later, after the boys had graduated from high school, I found several of the transplanted seedlings in juvenile stage, still growing furiously. Despite all odds they'd survived. Sometimes you just can't explain it, that persistence. I think of this tree farm now and how our boys have grown up. The odds they've faced.

We baby boomer parents are a select group, highly educated and forever in the spotlight, even for the way we're raising our children. Our parents sacrificed for us and under their guidance, we toted pennies in brown manila envelopes to our school savings programs (whatever happened to that money, by the way?). Such training by our parents pushed us to also want the best for our offspring, and some say that we've spoiled them. Recently, while I was conversing with another parent, she commented to me, "I don't know what our kids are doing. They seem to plug into society later than we did. They're waiting longer to choose a career, longer to select a partner, longer to support themselves."

"Right," I agree, "they don't want to be plugged-in. They want an extension cord."

And I mean it. Our kids don't have to face a military draft (yet) or the Depression (yet) or other adrenalin-type eras where people put survival before hedonism. Not yet. Their abuses or dalliances could be considered frivolous. One could think our offspring would be much more enlightened with the "Be Here Now/Turn On, Tune In, Drop Out" philosophy we parents so embraced (at least some of us). Others of us didn't "turn on" but still had lofty hopes and dreams for our kids. And we vowed to bring an improved world to our children along with the discretional luxury to choose the *best* from life. If any parents could manage to do it, we would, living in a nation of plenty and on the *Sputnik* launching pad of enterprise and opportunity. But no matter what generation, even back to the Dust Bowl or Great Gatsby parties (or whatever era we want to consider as either painful or glamorous), there has always existed the disease of alcoholism. And we still have its lugubrious effects filtering drip-by-numbing-drip down through the generations— perhaps a major factor for the past legislation of Prohibition. (But everyone knows that idea was a failure. How we love to break a rule if someone will just write it out for us!) These days we're living longer and longer; we have so much time to make mistakes now; to become addicted.

The good news is that we also have time to correct our mistakes. Every individual is eligible for the hope of sobriety and productivity. Thank goodness we have tools to help us through our humanness. They are innumerable, varied and individual, and perhaps there is one which will serve each of us.

With sobriety on the platter, I wonder what our next family holiday will be like. I question how we'll set up our household to withstand the odds of relapse and how we will survive it. Our extended family generally does not include much alcohol at family gatherings. It has never been an emphasis. And besides, it's not my problem...keeping my son sober. It's his. I have to let go.

"I don't think that anyone can understand powerlessness until it's way too late," Toren comments. He says this while Don and I are visiting him in early December at his halfway house in Florida. He's been there about one month and we're talking about his fall into alcoholism and how he climbed back out. He equates it to struggling in a riptide...being pulled out to sea, giving up to powerlessness, and going with the currents down the shore until you've regained enough strength to swim back in. Then, you swim *with* the rip. You quit fighting and go with it, knowing its strength. But you don't give up. You maintain your sense of self.

Within our family, we now have courage to talk about alcoholism and binge drinking. A common phone question: "Did you party this weekend?" It's easily asked to the brothers because the disease is with us. We acknowledge it, watch it closely, and treasure our closeness. Drinking is now considered as dangerous as a bad sunburn—a weekend souvenir that can progress to death, the beginning of a haunting cancer.

Toren's brothers tell me they plan to visit Toren at his halfway house in the spring. I recall what the rehab therapist warned about "the brothers" so we discuss with them the importance of continuing a non-drinking family atmosphere, at least while Toren is in his first year of sobriety. Even if Toren says we can drink around him, abstaining is a symbol of our awareness and support. Toren's brothers agree with this idea and answer that it is not the slightest problem for them. Don and I wonder if they are drinking less alcohol now that they have had the chance to become more educated about the chronic progressive symptoms of alcoholism and our family's genetic background. We don't know; they live too far away and we only see them once or twice a year. But because of what we have been through, it is easy to bring it up, easy to question not only the routine of their younger brother, but all our lifestyles. Each of us is fair game now. But Toren reminds me, "What my friends and family do about their drinking is up to them. I'm busy taking care of me."

Talking about one of his friends, Toren comments, "She doesn't understand how I can't just go have one beer. She wasn't trying to talk me into anything. But I can see that she doesn't get it. I said to her, 'I've never done one beer. I do *all* the beer. You might as well give me all of it. I *never* drank a beer just to drink *a* beer. One beer never benefited me.'" Toren goes on to say this is a great deterrent for him. He never needs to drink again since one single beer isn't his style. "If I can remember that," he grins, "I'm set."

I ask him about years down the road, how he can face never having a drink. He's suddenly quiet. I see that it's overwhelming for him to contemplate.

"I can't think about the future," Toren answers. "I just think about today, that I don't need to drink today. The rest of my life is almost too much to fathom."

Toren is fragile. I see he has undergone a transition that has left him translucent. In the past, he always seemed to know everything and would announce his destination with determination (even if, in reality, he wasn't headed there.) Now he's telling me that he lives for "just now." In the present. He's pliable, recovering. I remind myself to let up, to not push him. It surprises me that he seems incapable of looking ahead. He senses this and reassures me that the program emphasizes making it through each day. Otherwise, for someone that age, a whole lifetime might be too much to promise, a set-up for failure.

"What do you think about the rules at your halfway house?" I ask him.

Toren smiles. "They're a safety net. I don't have to worry about messing up. There's no temptation around here."

Toren is referring to the simple regulations required by his halfway program: house rules. Staffed with an advisory/consulting board of psychotherapists and a physician, the sober living program where Toren resides requires a daily curfew, attendance at meetings and commitment to a recovery program, full-time work or school, and agreement to behavioral, language, and grooming standards. Possession or use of alcohol, drugs, mood-altering substances or paraphernalia is prohibited. Residents must attend a weekly meeting of all occupants. The apartments house over eighty recovering addicts, all graduates of various inpatient rehab programs. Smoking is permitted only outdoors. No persons other than the residents and staff are allowed on the premises (this means no visitors or girlfriends). The apartment complex provides two bedroom/two bath facilities with TV, dishwasher, swimming pool, exercise room, tennis courts and Jacuzzi, as well as towels, kitchenware and linens, utilities and phone. Each resident shares a room with a roommate so that four persons occupy an apartment. Toren was able to move in with minimal possessions, search for a job, open a bank account, and begin his sober regime.

"I'm so happy to be functioning in a normal life," Toren says. He goes on to explain, "Our first night at the halfway house, some of my roommates and I went to a meeting. Then afterwards, we went into a sports bar. I *never* thought we'd go to a place like that. We ordered bottled waters and soft drinks, food and snacks, and watched football games while we laughed and talked." Toren smiles. "It was just like things could be, without drinking."

Toren is looking for a job, eager to be busy. He explains to me that many recovering alcoholics face discrimination and hardship when looking for work. Some people in recovery have never before held down a job successfully. Toren adds, "The attitude of the counselors at the halfway house is, if you can work without getting high or drinking, it's a miracle. I know I can." Toren faces a unique situation. He is transitioning from having lived in a foreign culture for almost a year, to a highly structured rehab environment, to the relative freedom of an apartment and to basic ground rules. Thankfully, holding down a job is nothing new to Toren. He figures it's a matter of time before he finds one. Toren has lived on his own as well, but never without his former closest companion, alcohol.

Living on the opposite side of the U.S. will be a fresh experience for Toren. He says he is content to find a new life, he is ready to move on from his days in South America. As an indication of his mental transition, Toren calls his former neighbor in the tiny village to talk with her about his remaining possessions. They decide to raffle off his refrigerator with proceeds going to the village school. He discusses with her who should get his furniture and his most valuable items and describes what articles he wants shipped home. Toren tells her honestly about his disease and his difficulties with alcohol. She certainly understands because alcoholism is a problem for people in her family, as well. Toren tells me that he feels great satisfaction finally communicating with her after having departed from his village so abruptly.

"I called some of my old school friends. They took it better than I thought." Toren talks about informing past high school and college buddies, "They didn't give me a hard time. I don't know if they really understand it, but at least they still want to be my friends.

I don't know if I can see them for a long time, though. It's never going to be the same." He looks disappointed. When phoning Chad, one of his former high school friends, Toren discovers Chad is presently in alcohol rehab as well. He suggests I talk with his Chad's mother. Toren jokes, "When I go to my high school reunion, my friends and I can attend our meetings together while you moms go to yours."

It takes all kinds of people to combat alcoholism. I get ahold of Chad's mother and, to my surprise, she divulges that her former husband was an alcoholic. For years I'd dropped Toren off at their house, never knowing. Alcoholism is truly a non-discriminating disease, not a disease of character. All kinds of people are affected by it. It attacks without discrimination.

There is another thing on my mind as we visit Toren at his halfway program. I have read what Toren writes, I know him in my heart, but I do not hear him talking much about remorse or regret except that he was not able to finish his work in South America. Perhaps expressing apology isn't necessary if Toren sees that his former life didn't work and is motivated to move on. His actions will now do the talking. But if Toren insists he has no regrets, what does this say about his attitude towards other people in his life? For example, does he not regret treatment of his high school administrators, coaches, and fellow teammates when he was expelled? Does he not regret his disrespect of the RD in college (yes, the RD was only doing his job but he does have feelings); the horse cart driver in South America who faced a damaged cart; the campus police who were obligated to shadow him and shine lights onto his balcony (surely they had other things to do); the hapless custodian who had to clean up the burned-out trash can; any miscellaneous persons he might have offended and can't even remember? How can he not regret the inconvenience and nuisance he inflicted upon these people?

The sober Toren I've known is not a person who would harm someone thoughtlessly. At one time, when I saw his reluctance to express remorse, I would have said, "How can Toren do this to me?" But now I say, "How can Toren do this to himself?" Since this issue has not resolved itself, I can only await more understanding, for both of us.

When Toren talks with me about turning points in his awareness of alcoholism, he mentions two distinct stories which impacted him. The first story was when I confided to him about Dustin, my friend's son who had to be brought home from college because he was experiencing seizures as a result of chronic alcohol abuse. Toren reminds me that this story caused him to think about his drinking experiences and it haunted him during his self-detox sessions when he feared that he, too, would have a seizure. The other reoccurring image that Toren could not shake was a story I'd told him about my high school reunions, how at ten years, twenty years, and thirty years, there had always been "the class drunk" who hit on all the women, fell down dancing and generally made a fool of himself (yes, it was usually a male, but by the thirty year reunion, there was a female, as well.) Toren reveals, "I heard those stories and said, 'That could be me. I could be that person at our class reunion.'" And he did not want it to come true.

"But what can be done before it's too late?" I ask Toren. I want to encourage others out there, suggest something that would really make a difference in their drinking choices.

"Talk to kids about their drinking habits. Threats won't work, but education about alcohol, what can happen with alcoholism as a disease, about family genetics and family patterns of drinking...all this helps." Toren stresses, "Kids need to know what the red flags are. They should be warned and educated rather than punished or threatened. The punishments make it into a 'Them vs. Us' situation."

"Do you mean in high school?"

Toren tells me, "In my case, it was more in college, because that's when I was doing my heaviest drinking. That's when people like me develop drinking problems. That's when I needed more emphasis. Punishment doesn't do jack shit."

Warn kids about the future, about the potential for disaster. That's what Toren says we should do. At least, that's what he tells us now, in retrospect. I think of the warnings he did receive from his RD in the dorm; the requirement to attend AA meetings in the summer. This was a way to educate Toren and it did impact him, even though he did not fulfill the entire "punishment." Some information filtered through. But it took a few more years of abuse before Toren sought help. To me, it seems there must be more definitive methods. I research this area and discover several curricula written for counselors and health care professionals to reduce high risk drinking among college students. One in particular has exacting protocol. It is published by the National Institute on Alcohol Abuse and Alcoholism (NIAAA), and considers changes in alcohol use after intervention and education.[63] The guidelines for using brief intervention state:

- ✓ All students who drink above recommended limits of alcohol use should receive brief intervention.
- ✓ Students who are resistant or who fail brief intervention may have a more serious problem than first suspected and should be referred to an alcohol treatment specialist.
- ✓ Change is a long-term process, not a single event. Physicians may have to speak with students on many occasions before they are ready to change behavior.

There we have it. Even professionals acknowledge that changing drinking behavior is a lengthy process. When they say it, it sounds reassuring. But when we experience it, the lengthy wait for a different behavior seems endless.

In the March 15, 2004, *USA Today,* there is an interview with undergraduates who talk about campus drinking. One of their suggestions is to involve students in the decision making about campus alcohol problems. It seems that more and more students are sensing the need for reform and tougher penalties for those who violate campus alcohol policies.[64]

As students look at drinking, their parents may be forced to join in. The most up-to-date research is showing that even heavy social drinkers who are not in treatment but function relatively well in the community exhibit the same patterns of brain damage as seen in hospitalized alcoholics. Brain scans show enough damage to impair day-to-day functioning in balance and reading. Apparently, to fall into this category, men must consume an average of one hundred drinks per month and women must consume an average of eighty per month.[65]

From Washington State, I mailed Toren the first portion of the manuscript for *Our Drink*. It was mid-November and he was still in his first weeks at the halfway program; he had been sending his chapters to me on the Internet from the library. For the first time, Toren saw what I was writing and, for the first time, he read our combined work. He did not call me back for several days. When he finally phoned, he confessed, "Reading what we wrote sucked a lot of energy out of me. I never knew what a dark moment it was in my life. I can't believe what I was doing—and over and over again. It's called 'dumb-ass.' I never realized how my actions were affecting so many people besides myself. I was just doing things for me. I was sinking."

As I listened to Toren say this, tears welled in my eyes. Toren has always possessed an optimistic personality that overlooked bad things and moved on. Maybe this hurt him because he diminished the harm of his actions. I've always joked about an image of Toren submerged in the bay with bricks strapped onto his feet, gurgling all the way down, blurting, "Oh look, there's a species of crab I've never seen! And look at the fabulous colors, the way the light filters through the water! Even though I'm surely suffocating and will soon die, this's a marvelous experience. I never could've had this insight if I weren't drowning!" Or sinking. As he just admitted.

But this same optimism probably pulled Toren out of the clutches of the disease when he insisted, "Yes, I deserve happiness. Now I'm seeing my life turning dark. I want my life back. I will get it back. I will have it. It's mine."

What saved our son? I think it was that, ultimately, he possessed a combination of his own determination and our love. He cherished his good fortune even as he made poor decisions, and then he used his desire to stop drinking to make his life better. My husband has always maintained that "Luck happens when preparation meets opportunity." Perhaps Toren's years of missteps were leading him to the opportunity to find himself. Toren listened to what people said even though he did otherwise. When at last his life became unmanageable, he had the fortitude to bail out. All these qualities added up to his enlightenment. Here was a kid who continued to take risks and who continued to self destruct while his parents persisted in pointing out bad patterns and pushed for better behavior. It was not a miracle combination. It was a mishmash of luck, effort, education and readiness. All this paid off.

So what is the plan to fix this world's problem with alcohol? Like rehab, each person has to deal with it individually, each family. And our nation must face it as well—educating people about the costs and consequences of alcohol consumption. It's not a disease we can Band-Aid. Battling alcoholism and addiction takes a personal strategy. It requires awareness of the progressive effects and the courage to bring it up even through pain. If we work for gravy it might be there. We forge ahead through love and guts.

23

Clinically Obsessed

Late January 2004. I'll never be given enough time to figure this all out. As it stands right now, since trudging up the stairs to the Peace Corps nurse, I'm going into my fifth month of sobriety (hold applause). With this little amount of time to reflect, I can only say that I'm always going to be evaluating my life and my conclusions will probably evolve. Reading back through all that we've written has been extremely exhausting for me. What started as innocent journal-writing (where I first sprang a leak and began investigating the reality of my drinking progression) has turned my life backwards and brought about this literary compilation.

Many volunteers go into the Peace Corps for two years hoping to gain life experience, contribute to humanity, and come out with a better understanding of themselves and another culture. As it turns out I have achieved these things in a far less amount of time and in a very skewed manner. In South America, amidst a foreign environment, my alcohol problems were completely unmasked and shortly thereafter in rehab, I found myself facing a different culture than most volunteers anticipate: one where people want to, try to, and often struggle to be sober.

I've come to much more of an understanding about my situation. Up to this point, my writing has served its purpose largely as a therapeutic release and as a means of reflection. There have been times that I go over what I have written and wonder: what is the point? Or, who cares? Sometimes I think it just sounds vain. What started out as a desperate inquiry scribbled into my journal has now expanded and exposed my experiences with drinking from start to finish.

This isn't an autobiography or an attempt to reveal the depth of or lack of my character. In fact, this is really an attempt to portray how alcohol has affected me personally and how I have come to understand what alcoholism means to me: the drunk-ass alcoholic. Every alcoholic's version of this would differ from mine in lots of ways, but there would be many underlying similarities accentuated by the disease's ability to manifest itself in all kinds of personalities and its capability to lead the afflicted through a worsening progression, one which ends with either sobriety or more commonly with jail, institutions, and death.

I have attempted to keep the focus of this story primarily based on my experiences with alcohol and how I got to where I am today. This self-serving, premature memoir-in-a-bottle may be something that someone else can relate to, appreciate, or learn from, so it may potentially be of use to people other than my family and me. In no way is this a crusade against my past or the abuse of alcohol because it would be silly of me to try to alter the course of either.

The first time I spoke with my parents on the phone in Washington, D.C., and told them about my drinking difficulties and what I was suddenly doing back in the United States, I felt about 1000 pounds of pressure lifted off my back. Finally, I was no longer burdened with my secrets. (I had debated mentioning my struggles to them earlier while I was studying in Mexico or perhaps when they would have come to visit me in my village the following May in South America.) Having put myself out there and confronted my problem, I no longer had anything else inside eating me up. All the feelings and internal struggles no longer had to be suppressed, stuffed away or silently borne.

By now, I don't have much left to hide. Everything has been dragged to the surface and I'm allowed to properly deal with and, hopefully, discard what was beginning to plague me. The odd part about all of this is, if I had known the 'clinical severity' of my problem as seen through the eyes of the professionals, there is absolutely no way I would have so clumsily turned myself in and asked for help. None of this was what I was intending or hoping for. All I knew was that things were worsening fast and I was desperate.

Luckily I was 'semi-buzzed' and didn't think about all of the procedural repercussions that would follow. There was nobody more sure than I that I'd found my village home for the next two years and that I would be happily working in South America during that period of time.

The drastic jolt of being forced to leave South America, that inverse culture shock, transported me quickly from my mellow, third-world haven into a cutting-edge rehab facility. Over the previous nine months, I had surrendered much of my self-identity by mixing into my foreign village community. It had taken a long time for me to achieve a sense of acceptance and I had finally forged close relationships between myself and some of the families. To be torn so quickly from all this, and suddenly find myself sitting on an office chair in a semi-circle sharing about feelings, acceptance and powerlessness with other men was something I hope I will only experience once.

At that point, my reality was nothing believable. To me, life had become surreal. Within a period of six days I had confessed in a nurse's office and then detoxed in a hotel room; I had traveled across South American dirt roads to pull my belongings from my village; I had squatted two nights in a hotel in Washington, D.C., while being questioned and assessed by all kinds of counselors; and now I had succumbed to a northeastern U.S. rehab center. My soul still remained back in my village. Through all the confusion, my alcohol problem was the one thing that was still with me.

All of this happened with few decisions being made by me, which is probably what allowed it to take place. There was no point that I was allowed to step backwards and withdraw my previous statements or reconsider the direction I was going. It was too late. The term 'rock bottom' is relative, but being so desperate that I traded in my whole world without resistance reflects the bankruptcy that I was experiencing inside. These feelings of despair are the same ones that allowed me to continue listening to outside help and intervening suggestions. As opposed to all the times before when 'in trouble' with my parents or authorities, this time I was ready to look at options. Losing my would-be life in South America allowed me to gain perspective on the seriousness of my situation and also made it difficult to hide from anyone.

Surely, when my friends see me they'll wonder, "Wasn't he supposed to be in South America for another year-and-a-half?" This significant turning point allowed me to get honest with myself and everyone else, in order to start identifying what now seems like the beginning of a nightmare, one that I somehow had awakened from.

Near the end of rehab, I was given choices for what they call 'aftercare'—where to go and what to do afterwards. This was packaged with a strong recommendation for me to live in a halfway house.

"What? Are you crazy?"

My therapist kindly pointed out to me that I didn't have any clue how to live like a normal adult in society. College didn't count. She then reminded me of my eight continuous months of drinking spanning from my May 2002 college graduation to my studies in Mexico, prior to my trip of self-discovery with the Peace Corps in 2003.

"Ooooh, right, thaaat." It was a painful realization, just how correct she was, and that she knew what she was talking about, partially due to my incriminating honesty. I was prime halfway house material.

Now, in late January of 2004, being a little over three months into my approximately six-month stay in the halfway house, I've been a sort of blank slate. It's similar to how I felt when I arrived at my village in South America. The difference is that this time for a supporting community, I have a bunch of sick, mentally-impoverished addicts, replacing the rural farming community that formerly had me as their struggling volunteer. In this halfway environment, I am no longer searching for a functional way to socially drink. Opting to be in a corner of the United States where I know next to nobody, I have had plenty of face time with myself to think it all through, lick my wounds, and react to a new emerging lifestyle, one that I'm not sure anyone like me can completely embrace from the get-go. Bored, bored, boredboredboredbored.

Hesitant to accept that I will always be sober and never again be drinking, I have learned to try to focus more on each day as it comes. I try to worry less about all of the times I will be the shoo-in designated driver and all the times I may be counted on to clarify blurry details of upcoming nights. People will still drink, I guess—just not me.

I have noticed several differences in a sober me today. Some make me question myself and wonder if I have completely sold out and turned into this sissy recovering alcoholic who is overly open about his problems. But there are changes in my life I have appreciated. I have noticed that I'm no longer 'living to drink,' and more importantly as it was quickly becoming, 'drinking to live.' Increasingly, my life revolved around the time that I was drunk; the time that I was sober counted less and less. It had come to the point that I only put up with sobriety. Instead, I looked for the next chance to get liquored-up and disappear into oblivion—just waiting to drink all the time. Now I'm no longer just going through the motions with a bottle or tall can lingering in the back of my mind. I have no strings attached to my next 'good time' and I can be more in the moment and give myself to the situation.

It's not to say that I don't miss a lot of the good fun that came with drinking, but I am able to appreciate my time much more without weighing it against exaggerated extremes or having to wait out real life so I can go crazy for a few days. My existence used to operate on a basis of rewards. I was always fulfilling a 'requirement' in order to earn the next chance to drink and have fun. Most people operate on a basis of personal rewards but, by the end, my system became reliant only on alcohol. I was most concerned about drinking and, therefore, unable to put myself towards anything else. On one side you could say I was 'clinically obsessed' with alcohol, even when I wasn't drunk or physically exposed, my body anticipated it and my brain looked for the next opportunity to blissfully self-destruct.

Sobriety has definitely shown me much more of a stable version of reality. Gone are the times that I lived for during the better part of the last nine years. Being one who appreciates a taste of chaos, spontaneity and excitement, this new tranquil consistency is almost traumatic. If it weren't for days of guitar playing and simple living down in South America to cushion this unforeseen transition, I may have had more difficulty. I no longer look to the weekends as a source of endless drinks, wild late nights, memory lapses into oblivion, and the subsequent loss of inhibition and control that were so normal to me. I no longer face waking up to shakes and sweats, dehydration or any of the total confusion, insanity or regret that used to follow a typical benchmark evening. Also gone is the absurdity, hilarity, lunacy and knee-slapping silliness that I always counted on. Where can I still find some of that?

24

Dry Run

Dear Toren,

You speak of your halfway experience as dull. Monotonous. Mind-numbing. The ennui of boredom can be a form of simplicity, a rehearsal for being ready to make the next step. It's the repetition of doing undemanding things right, having them turn out in simple form, then being prepared to face added frustration and complications without falling back into old habits.

In the halfway situation, layers and seasonings have been stripped from your life. You are geared down to essentials. Gone are your gadgets, posters on the wall, email contacts, friends and social schedules. Your Peace Corps work, which was meaningful and inspiring to you, has vanished. In its place is tedious, unrewarding work. Therefore, your life has the appearance of being dreary and lackluster. But you are not a boring or uninspired person in reality. You must remember this as you repeat again and again waking up, going to work, then repeating again. You are building muscle memory to walk you through the next steps. This gives you rhythm before you add chords or elaborate riffs.

At the halfway house, you are preparing, just as you do in any school, for the chance to continue on. What appears to lack depth and flavor is like practicing musical scales, going over them until you can perform them in your sleep perfectly, three octaves. Then one day when you have a meaningful choice, *you are ready. You will flourish. In any key.*

You, the real Toren behind the halfway shell, are still there practicing without distraction, looking at yourself over and over and over in the mirror after returning home at curfew, deciding how you will set off onto the next phase. You need this time to heal, to forgive, and to nurture your spirit without the interruption of all those people who would unduly influence, mistakenly guide, or destroy your concentration. You must do this on your own. You still possess the same substantial capabilities. But in the privacy of the halfway house, you don't feel the pseudo-pressure to act (as you have so aptly put it) "all happy, skippy or preachy, as though I have finally conquered the world."

It's not a production for someone else. What you are doing is just for you.

You know your disease is still with you. But you are stabilizing yourself so that you will someday be able to carry it on your shoulder without it concerning or distracting you. You are devising who you are, repositioning the load and looking forward to the time when you move on, lugging this thing which, in reality, no one will notice. To you it will be like an old scar, of no current consequence or power, but there as a reminder of what you refuse to become.

Love,

mom

25

Breaking the Sober-Ice

February 2004. At Christmastime, I had the chance to fly home for a few days and test uncharted territory—the old stomping ground—without alcohol, without the crutch-like supervision of my halfway house rules and regulations. I was extremely anxious about re-entry into my old life with everything turned upside down, not being able to converse normally with anyone because of all of the 'things' that were going on in my life—sent home from Peace Corps, put into rehab, not drinking, living in a halfway house in Florida.

"Hey, great to see you, too. Happy Holidays! Cheers!"

I found that a lot of this struggle was really in *my* mind more than everyone else's. As it turns out, not everyone is dwelling on my misfortunes and thinking about my circumstances 90 percent of the time—if at all. It is all in my mind.

Whether I should return home so early in my halfway experience was a decision I wondered about. I wanted to go, but at the same time, I dreaded it. Some things are inevitable and the pain of anticipation, once again, proved to be far greater than the actual events experienced. I knew I was going to see all my old friends and familiar situations and would have the option of putting myself into potentially dangerous positions. I had many angles to think about. People in the rooms of recovery say, "If you want to be miserable, go hang out with a bunch of people who are drinking." Others take it to the next level and say, "If you hang around in a barber shop long enough, eventually you'll get a haircut."

I finally got to face my family, friends of the family, and all my friends and brothers' friends—all of the people who drove me to drink for so long. Right!! Basically, I feared that I'd have to constantly explain myself, tell people where I'm at and re-establish whatever I had going before I chose to disappear South. I worried that I would have to justify my not drinking, or make excuses as to why I couldn't drink to people who had always partied with me. I was afraid that they'd think I was betraying them or that they'd say I'd changed. The second part can't be denied. I had to change. What I found out was that people were not expecting explanations, nor were they waiting for me to break down and cry myself a drink. I guess my actions and living arrangements spoke for me more than anything. I felt acceptance and understanding, that people were still happy to see me, like anytime—drink or no drink.

Upon my arrival home I noticed that there was NO alcohol in our usually diversely-stocked fridge. The liquor cabinet was practically dead-bolted and the once all-too-vulnerable wine cellar was now mysteriously locked. "Oooh, yeah..." I was reminded, "their drunken son has come home for the first time." What a special feeling. The 'Dry Christmas' (something I guess I should get used to...boooooooring). Really, it was no big deal for me and our family in terms of our time spent together. Socializing with our relatives has never been about drinking either. I was concerned about feeling a sense of moral inferiority, but once again there was no reason for this because I was embraced warmly by the entire family.

My parents, brothers and I spent some time at home and then took off for a few days snow skiing; we were all just the same together, jokingly sarcastic as always. We discovered what could now pass as funny/offensive on our newly-installed Alco-Sensitivity meter. What can be said and what can't? Who cares? I'm the only one with weak willpower and a drinking problem. *HA!!* That was funny wasn't it? Halfway.

Against the recommendations of numerous voices of wisdom in recovery, I went out several nights and saw my 'old friends' and put myself in 'old places'—all situations where my disease would most likely want me to be. One could say that being in early recovery means that I have a very tenuous hold on sobriety. But I don't sit around wishing I could drink all the time. For almost a full year from even before the time I began working in South America, my body and mind were completely at odds with alcohol and I was slowly torturing myself to the point of complete surrender and defeat: the point of asking for help. This long process didn't just disappear from my conscience. Many things still come to mind when I think about alcohol and drinking in general, but when it comes to those things and *me,* it is very easy to remind myself about the pain and aftermath of alcohol and its recent effects on me. These reminders make being the designated driver seem like not that bad of a deal in comparison.

My first night out was a shock. I went to a house party with a friend and one brother. In preparation, we had agreed that we would leave the party at my first inkling of discomfort. All of us wanted my experience to be successful. I found myself at a larger-than-anticipated gathering with seemingly everybody I could think of that my therapist in rehab had said I would need to avoid. After getting past the initial distress of really being back and no longer under the illusion that living in Florida was an extension of my excursion to South America, I began to talk with people, searching for common ground and dealing with my new empty-handed antics. As I conversed with people, my eyes were overwhelmed with the beer cans in everybody's hands. Not having been around alcohol for three months was strange enough, but this abrupt reversal of over-stimulation was more than my sheltered brain could absorb.

Taking a panoramic scan of the room, all I saw were blurry images of people with cans and bottles popping out of their grasp. With every person I talked to, I had to make an enormous effort not to let my eyes wander down to stare at their beers. I felt like a little puppy that couldn't stop begging for food; my eyes just couldn't get past the beer. The sensation felt similar to when you're wearing an itchy wool cap and you're searching for your lost keys: you're hot, frustrated, preoccupied. It literally took an hour or two until I began to feel comfortable, until I could quit sweating.

From that point on, I began to enjoy myself and adapted to this new form of so-called 'socializing.' By the end of the night, I was ecstatic to see everyone, to have a good time, and to know I was not going to suffer like I had in recent years from my progressing alcoholic disaster.

After that evening, I was not at all hesitant to go out the

remaining nights I spent in town seeing old friends. I even found myself in a few bars here and there without much temptation or discomfort. "You hang around in a barbershop long enough, you're gonna get a haircut." Maybe so, but I doubt that a cancer patient already bald from life-threatening chemotherapy would.

I noticed a lot of things about my social excursions with friends. The first and most important is this: it didn't make much of a difference that I wasn't drinking. What was striking to me was that most people weren't getting extremely intoxicated. So many of my party years had been about getting wasted. And eventually there was the other side of that curb I had to worry about—*not* getting *too* wasted. The big difference is that I no longer need to have any of this on my mind. There was no voice telling me I needed another drink before I do this or that, or that I needed a drink just to feel better. Nor was there a voice telling me, "You better slow down!" or the voice that warns, "You're gonna be gone soon!"

For the first time in years, I really didn't rely on alcohol to make me say or do things that I normally wouldn't. From the moment I went out until I got home, everything stayed the same. I experienced longer-than-usual nights where my 'buzz' never came and nothing ever changed. I was consistently either stimulated or unprovoked based solely on my natural response to a given circumstance. Neither did I go through those all-too-comforting, euphoric feelings that used to keep me coming back. In return, I got the sanity of knowing I was no longer screwing myself over on the inside. There was no internal conflict. No anticipation. No anxiety of withdrawals. I was fine with that. I'd never known that the solution to my drinking problem was to NOT drink. Damn it.

Going out and seeing everybody and breaking the 'sober-ice' was definitely necessary for me. I got that out of the way and now I can continue on, knowing that the world didn't end because I can't drink. I realize that most of my friends don't feel betrayed, aren't giving me the old, "You've changed, man," or whatever I thought would cave in everything I used to care about. There's no doubt that I feel a disconnection from my past and from my friends. But that probably would have happened to anyone who was out of the country for virtually a year, not to mention coming from a plan gone awry and living in a halfway house. What a bummer.

Back in Florida, I'm once again strapping on the training wheels for another four months to live out my commitment of a six-month stay. More than anything, I've been given this time as yet another opportunity to test my growing patience. Living under a constant curfew, having people check to see if I make my bed daily, confirming that I'm in bed every night are just some of the little things that try me. The real joys of the halfway house come from living in an apartment with three other strangers, guys who don't easily get along with each other and whose only commonality is that their pasts crumbled and brought them together in the wake of their own personal downfalls. Learning what is best for me may not always be what I want; it's a character-building experience, right?

I now come to face the whole idea of, "Okay, so I keep waking up and it's not a dream. I'm still not in South America as planned, and I am still not drinking." Both still seem so unreal. The last time I checked, those were my two short-term reasons for living: working in South America and drinking. I'm not about to pretend that I have suddenly stumbled onto the meaning of life just because I've forced myself to sober up. Actually, I feel like I'm still wiping my eyes and trying to figure things out. (What do I do with myself?) The one constant that fueled my social life and everything I chose to do and enjoy has been removed from my reach and suddenly I'm dealing with a whole new reality rather than slowly self-destructing. What do I do with all this time and energy?

I'm still not sure. Similar to 'out of control,' the term 'normal' is a relative and subjective term. I don't know what normal necessarily is, but what seems normal to me is abnormal, and what normal people do seems boring to me. I have a hard time knowing how to go about changing, eliminating, or replacing my behaviors with others when much of what I used to do seems like an all-or-nothing package deal.

Immeasurable results, I'm sure, will come through the loss of my Peace Corps experience and realization of my alcoholism. It appears this process and 're-evaluation' of my life won't ever end. Some wise man may say that, "Every time a door closes, a window opens." But that window might not look as sparkling as it sounds for the person who has to climb through it.

I'm tackling my problems just as many people have dealt with their own predicaments: by facing them. The severity of my physical reaction to alcohol forced me to confront my dilemma at a relatively early age, and I feel fortunate that this did not drag on for another decade. Some people never find the Twelve Steps or recover at all.

Where this will take me is not my big concern, as long as my journey isn't a loop. Along the way, the more I seem to learn, the less I feel I know. My existing halfway situation has given me a whole new model of living, a new focus. Today, I live more for the present. Words like powerlessness, acceptance, and willingness are etched into my latest vocabulary.

My 'rehearsal days' in the halfway house will eventually come to a close. I'm putting in the footwork so that I will have a foundation of recovery, a grasp on sobriety, and I will be able to get on with my life, whatever that may entail. By remaining honest with myself, by leaning on the 12-Step Program and by using my friends and family for support, I am given a second chance to move into unmarked chapters.

My story will continue to unfold. The disease will forever be with me (and with many other people). All I can do is use what I have learned to take responsibility for myself. It is all up to me. At my age, I am lucky. Now there is nothing in the way.

⊙urDrink
Communication Gauge™

The *Our Drink Communication Gauge* is a quick aid for families and teens to determine whether they are adequately informed about drinking choices. Use the reminders below to cover essential elements of alcohol awareness.

Using this gauge, you will create:

Openness	among family and friends
Understanding	of alcohol issues
Reality	of alcohol's influence in our world

Don't forget to discuss these *Our Drink* topics:

Dealing with relationships	personal problems can arise with heavy drinking
Red Flags	problems at school and work, legal and financial difficulty, and drinking to get drunk are signs of abuse
Importance of family history	genetics play a huge role in alcoholism
Neuro-effects of drinking	the adolescent and young adult brain is extremely susceptible to permanent damage
Knowledge of alcoholism	it's a progressive disease that starts with the first sip

INDEX OF ALCOHOL REFERENCES AND RESOURCES

AS A NATIONAL GOAL, THE U.S. SURGEON GENERAL HAS ESTABLISHED A
50-PERCENT REDUCTION IN COLLEGE BINGE DRINKING
BY THE YEAR 2010.

Text References

1.   Kapner, Daniel Ari. "Infofacts Resources: Alcohol and Other Drugs on Campus-The Scope of the Problem," [3/15/04] as found at http://www.edc.org/hec/pubs/factsheets/scope.html

   Weschsler, H.; Lee, J.E.; Kuo, M; Seibring, M; Nelson, T. F.; and Lee, H. "Trends in College Binge Drinking during a Period of Increased Prevention Efforts: Findings from 4 Harvard School of Public Health Study Surveys, 1993-2001." *Journal of American College Health* 50: 203-217, 2002. For more information on CAS, visit www.hsph.harvard.edu/cas/

2.   Wechsler, H., J.E. Lee, M. Kuo, and H. Lee. "College Binge Drinking in the 1990's: A Continuing Problem- Results of the Harvard School of Public Health 1999 College Alcohol Study." *Journal of American College Health* 48.10 (2000): 199-210.

3.   Wechsler, Henry, and Bernice Wuethrich. *Dying to Drink: Confronting Binge Drinking on College Campuses.* New York City: Rodale, 2002

4.   Jones, Thom. *Cold Snap.* Boston: Little, Brown and Company, 1995.

5.   *AMA Alliance Today,* 1998.

6.   Brown, S.A., S.F. Tapert, E. Granholm, and D.C. Delis. "Neurocognitive Functioning of Adolescents: Effects of Protracted Alcohol Use." *Alcoholism: Clinical and Experimental Research* 24.2 (February 2000).

7.   Giedd, J. N. et al. "Brain Development during Childhood and Adolescence: A Longitudinal MRI Study." *Nature Neuroscience* 2:10 (October 1999).

8.   Kuhn, Cynthia , Scott Swartzwelder, Wilkie Wilson. *Buzzed: The Straight Facts about the Most Used and Abused Drugs from Alcohol to Ecstasy.* New York City: W. W. Norton & Company, 1998.

9.   U.S. Dept. of Health and Human Services. *Tenth Special Report to the U.S. Congress on Alcohol and Health: Highlights from Current Research.* Alexandria, VA: EEI, September 2000.

10.   "Young People and Alcohol." Summary of Findings from the American Academy of Pediatrics Survey: Teen Alcohol Consumption, American Academy of

Pediatrics, September 1998, as retrieved March 10, 2004 at Alcohol Policies Project http://www.cspinet.org/booze/alcyouth.html

11.   National Institute on Alcohol Abuse and Alcoholism. "Cognitive Impairment and Recovery from Alcoholism." *Alcohol Alert* 53 (July 2001).

12.   Crews, F. T., C.J. Braun, B. Hoplight, R. C. Switzer III, and D.J. Knapp. "Binge Ethanol Consumption Causes Differential Brain Damage in Young Adolescent Compared with Adult Rats." *Alcoholism: Clinical and Experimental Research* 24.11 (November 2000).

13.   "NIAAA Releases Estimates of Alcohol Abuse and Dependence." *Media Advisory*, March 17, 1995.

14.   Kuhn, Cynthia , Scott Swartzwelder, Wilkie Wilson. *Buzzed: The Straight Facts about the Most Used and Abused Drugs from Alcohol to Ecstasy*. New York City: W. W. Norton & Company, 1998.

15.   White, A. M., D. Jamieson-Drake, and H. S. Swartzwelder. "Prevalence and Correlates of Alcohol-Induced Blackouts among College Students." *Journal of American College Health*. In review.

16.   Wechsler, Henry, and Bernice Wuethrich. *Dying to Drink: Confronting Binge Drinking on College Campuses*. New York City: Rodale, 2002

17.   Kuhn, Cynthia , Scott Swartzwelder, Wilkie Wilson. *Buzzed: The Straight Facts about the Most Used and Abused Drugs from Alcohol to Ecstasy*. New York City: W. W. Norton & Company, 1998.

18.   Wechsler, H., G.W. Dowdall, G. Maenner, J. Gledill-Hoyt, and H. Lee. "Changes in Binge Drinking and Related Problems Among American College Students Between 1993 and 1997: Results of the Harvard School of Public Health College Alcohol Study: *Journal of American College Health* 47 (September 1998).

19.   Harvard School of Public Health College Alcohol Study (CAS), *Journal of Studies on Alcohol*, 1994-2004 and www.hsph.harvard.edu/cas a study website for higher education alcohol abuse research, H. Wechsler Director.

20.   Peterson, Vincent J., B. Nisenholz, G. Robinson. *A Nation Under the Influence: America's Addiction to Alcohol*. New York: Alyn & Bacon, 2003.

21.   Wechsler, Henry, and Bernice Wuethrich. *Dying to Drink: Confronting Binge Drinking on College Campuses*. New York City: Rodale, 2002, p. 188-9.

22.   Russell, Jane. *"Deception in Reporting About Alcohol,* as reported at http://www.jrussellshealth.com/alcben_paradox.html

23. "One-Third of College Students Have Alcohol Disorders." *Alcoholism & Drug Abuse Weekly*, June 17, 2002 as found at www.jointogether.org

24. "Screening and Assessing." CAGE, TWEAK, CUGE tests, resource center for changing the college drinking culture. Learn about research and innovative approaches to prevention with interactive tools for students and educators. [3/11/2004] as reported at NIAAA
http://www.collegedrinkingprevention.gov/Reports/trainingmanual/module_2.aspx

25. Harvard School of Public Health College Alcohol Study (CAS), *Journal of Studies on Alcohol*, 1994-2004 and www.hsph.harvard.edu/cas A study website for higher education alcohol abuse research, H. Wechsler Director.

26. Ennet, S.T., Tobler, N.S., Ringwalt, C.L. et al. How effective is drug abuse resistance education ? A meta-analysis of Project DARE outcome evaluations. *American Journal of Public Health*, 1994, 84(9), 1394-1401.

Ringwalt, D.L., Ennett, S.T., & Holt, K.D. An outcome evaluation of Project DARE. *Health Education Research: Theory and Practice*, 1991, 6, 327-337.

Rosenbaum, D.P., Flewelling, R.L., Bailey, S.L. et al. Cops in the Classroom: A longitudinal evaluation of drug abuse resistance education (DARE*). Journal of Research in Crime and Delinquency*, 1194, 31(1), 3-31.

27. "Gene May Be Linked to Binge-Drinking Behavior." *Alcohol and Alcoholism*, September 2003 as found at www.jointogether.org

28. Grant, B. "The Impact of Family History of Alcoholism on the Relationship between Age at Onset of Alcohol Use and DSM-IV Alcohol Dependence: Results from the National Longitudinal Alcohol Epidemiologic Survey: *Alcohol Health and Research World* 22.2 (1998): 144-47.

29. Carver, Raymond. *All of Us*. New York: Vintage Contemporaries, 2000.

30. Jellinek, E. M. *The Disease Concept of Alcoholism*. New Brunswick, NJ: Milhouse Press, 1960. *http://www.in.gov/judiciary/ijlap/issues/sub_abuse/jellinek.html*

31. The Doors. *Whiskey Bar* by Bert Brecht and Kurt Weill.

32. Wechsler, Henry, and Bernice Wuethrich. *Dying to Drink: Confronting Binge Drinking on College Campuses*. New York City: Rodale, 2002, p. 158.

33. Ochs, R. "Students Need Lesson in Alcohol Avoidance." *Los Angeles Times*, September 24, 2001: page S5.

34. Harvard School of Public Health College Alcohol Study (CAS), *Journal of*

Studies on Alcohol, 1994-2004 and www.hsph.harvard.edu/cas A study website for higher education alcohol abuse research. (2002), H. Wechsler, Director.

35.   Harvard School of Public Health College Alcohol Study (CAS), *Journal of Studies on Alcohol*, 1994-2004 and www.hsph.harvard.edu/cas A study website for higher education alcohol abuse research. (1999), H. Wechsler, Director.

36.   Wechsler, Henry, and Bernice Wuethrich. *Dying to Drink: Confronting Binge Drinking on College Campuses*. New York City: Rodale, 2002, p. 213.

37.   "Binge Drinking Costing Billions," BBC News UK Edition, September 19, 2003, as reported at http://news.bbc.co.uk/1/hi/health/3121440.stm

38.   United Nations Population Fund: UNFPA. "Supporting Adolescents & Youth," population issues as reported at http://www.unfpa.org/adolescents/

39.   "Binge Drinking Costing Billions," BBC News UK Edition, September 19, 2003, as reported at http://news.bbc.co.uk/1/hi/health/3121440.stm

40.   "Teen Drinking Sets Pattern for Life," September 7, 2003, The Study by the Centre for Adolescent Health at the Royal Children's Hospital, Australia, as reported at http://alcoholism.about.com/b/a/024359.htm

41.   "One-Third of College Students Have Alcohol Disorders." *Alcoholism & Drug Abuse Weekly*, June 17, 2002 as found at www.jointogether.org

42.   Wechsler, Henry, and Bernice Wuethrich. *Dying to Drink: Confronting Binge Drinking on College Campuses*. New York City: Rodale, 2002, p. 6.

43.   Russell, Jane. *"Deception in Reporting About Alcohol,* as reported at http://www.jrussellshealth.com/alcben_paradox.html

44.   Hingson, R., T. Heeren, R.C. Zakocs, A. Kopstein, and H. Wechsler. "Magnitude of Alcohol-Related Mortality and Morbidity Among U.S. College Students Ages 18-24." *Journal of Studies on Alcohol* 63.2 (April 12, 2002): 136-44.

45.   Koss, M.P., C.A. Gidycz and N. Wisniewski. "The Scope of Rape: Incidence and Prevalence of Sexual Aggression and Victimization in a National Sample of Higher Education Students." *Journal of Consulting and Clinical* Psychology 55 (1987): 162-70.

46.   Harvard School of Public Health College Alcohol Study (CAS), *Journal of Studies on Alcohol*, 1994-2004 and www.hsph.harvard.edu/cas A study website for higher education alcohol abuse research. (2004), H. Wechsler, Director.

47.   "Perception and Reality: A National Evaluation of Social Norms Marketing Interventions to Reduce College Students' Heavy Alcohol Use,*" Journal of Studies on*

Alcohol, 2003.

48.   Palmadesso, Daniel. "Harvard Study: Students Will Drink No Matter What," *Cornell Daily Sun,* September 9, 2003.

49.   Carver, Raymond. *All of Us.* New York: Vintage Contemporaries, 2000.

50.   Carver, Raymond. *All of Us.* New York: Vintage Contemporaries, 2000.

51.   Coontz, Stephanie. *The Way We Never Were.* New York: Basic Books, July 2000.

52.   Kuhn, Cynthia , Scott Swartzwelder, Wilkie Wilson. *Buzzed: The Straight Facts about the Most Used and Abused Drugs from Alcohol to Ecstasy.* New York City: W. W. Norton & Company, 1998.

53.   Troncale, Joseph, M.D. "Medical Aspects of the Disease of Addiction," Caron Foundation, Pennsylvania, October 17, 2003. www.caron.org

54.   Berke, J. D., and S. E. Hyman. Addiction, dopamine and molecular mechanisms of memory. *Neuron 25* (2000) 515-532.

55.   Kuhn, Cynthia , Scott Swartzwelder, Wilkie Wilson. *Buzzed: The Straight Facts about the Most Used and Abused Drugs from Alcohol to Ecstasy.* New York City: W. W. Norton & Company, 1998. p. 40.

56.   "How Far Can 12 Steps Go?" Lampman, Jane. *The Christian Science Monitor,* January 21, 2004, p. 12.

57.   Lemanski, M.J. (2000 January/February). Addiction alternatives for recovery. *Humanist,* 60(1), 14f.

58.   Polich, J. M.; D.J. Armor; H. B. Braiker. "Stability and Change in Drinking Patterns," *The Course of Alcoholism: Four Years After Treatment.* New York: John Wiley & Sons, 1981.

59.   Gordon, Susan Merle. "Relapse & Recovery: Behavioral Strategies for Change." The Caron Foundation, 2003. www.caron.org

60.   "Rush is Back on Air after Rehab." Johnson, Peter. *USA Today,* November 18, 2003.

61.   "Let Go." Source: Caron Foundation. www.caron.org

62.   Carver, Raymond. *All of Us.* New York: Vintage Contemporaries, 2000.

63.   "Clinical Protocols to Reduce High Risk Drinking in College Students."

National Institute on Alcohol Abuse and Alcoholism (NIAAA), September 2003. http://www.collegedrinkingprevention.gov/Reports/trainingmanual/contents.aspx

64. "Colleges Take Fresh Look at Putting Lid on Drinking." Marklein, Mary Beth. *USA Today*, March 15, 2004, p. 7D.

65. "Brain Damage from Heavy Social Drinking." Healy, Michelle, *USA Today*, April 15, 2004 as cited from *Alcoholism: Clinical and Experimental Research*, Dieter Meyerhoff at University of California.

A. A. Alcoholics Anonymous is worldwide with A.A. meetings in almost every community. You can find times and places of local A.A. meetings or events by looking in your telephone directory or using this link: www.alcoholics-anonymous.org

Ala-non/Alateen Your inquiry is confidential and anonymous. If you are concerned about someone else's drinking, browse the web site for information about the program. Call 888-4AL-ANON, Monday through Friday, 8 am to 6 pm ET for meeting information. WSO@al-anon.org

About Alcoholism What You Need to Know About Alcoholism/Substance Abuse, Articles links. http://alcoholism.about.com/cs/college

Alagna, Magdalena. *Everything You Need to Know About the Dangers of Binge Drinking.* New York: Rosen Publishing Group, 2001. (Geared to teens with reading difficulties.)

Alcohol 101 http://www.alcohol101plus.org/home.html Century Council interactive CD Rom exploring alcohol decisions in at-risk college settings.

Alcohol Policies Project http://cspinet.org/booze Advocacy for the prevention of alcohol problems.

AlcoholScreening.org Self-test offered on-line to assess drinking patterns, personalized feedback, links to support resources including a database of 12,000 treatment centers.

AlcoPRO Drug and Alcohol testing products for home use, P.O. Box 10954, Knoxville, TN 37939, 1-800-227-9890, www.alcopro.com

A Matter of Degree (AMOD) www.amodstrat.net College environment advocacy group that furthers changes in college life to reduce alcohol abuse.

Break Away www.alternativebreaks.org The mission is to promote alcohol-free spring break opportunities.

Caron Foundation. Excellence in Addiction Treatment. Adult and adolescent residential treatment. www.caron.org

"Clinical Protocols to Reduce High Risk Drinking in College Students." **National Institute on Alcohol Abuse and Alcoholism (NIAAA)**, September 2003, a curriculum for health care professionals to identify and treat at-risk students. http://www.collegedrinkingprevention.gov/Reports/trainingmanual/contents.aspx

DC, Center for Disease Control and Prevention, National Center for Chronic Disease Prevention & Health Promotion, *Trends Data for Alcohol Use and Chronic Drinking* grouped by categories, Department of Health and Human Services.

http://apps.nccd.cdc.gov/brfss/Trends/ trendchart.asp?state=US&qkey =10110&bkey =327048&grp=0&SUBMIT4=Go

CIRCLe Network www.circlenetwork.org A nonprofit group that works to improve campus life.

The CORE Institute www.coreinstitute.com A federally funded program assisting higher education with alcohol and drug prevention efforts, surveys, campus-based prevention programs.

Goldstein, A. *Addiction: From Biology to Drug Policy.* New York: W. H. Freeman, 1994.

Harvard School of Public Health College Alcohol Study (CAS) www.hsph.harvard.edu/cas A study website for higher education alcohol abuse research.

Higher Education Center for Alcohol and Other Drug Information (HEC) www.edc.org/hec HEC develops, implements and evaluates programs to reduce student problems related to alcohol, drugs and violence.

Jane Russell http://www.jrussellshealth.com/index.html Health Facts about alcohol consumption categorized under specific topics.

Jellinek, E. M. The Jellinek Curve http://www.in.gov/judiciary/ijlap/ issues/sub abuse/jellinek.html

Join Together www.jointogether.org People working to prevent substance abuse including a national directory, information, and funding sources.

Kuhn, Cynthia, Scott Swartzwelder, Wilkie Wilson. *Buzzed: The Straight Facts about the Most Used and Abused Drugs from Alcohol to Ecstasy.* New York City: W. W. Norton & Company, 1998.

The Marin Institute for the Prevention of Alcohol and Other Drug Problems www.marininstitute.org Focuses on environments that glamorize alcohol use including database about alcohol beverage industry, policies.

Mothers Against Drunk Driving (MADD) www.madd.org Provides group information and counseling for victims.

Michigan Alcohol Screening Test (MAST) A quickly administered questionnaire to determine signs of alcoholism. www.ncadd-sfv.org/ symptoms/mast test.html (see Appendix ii)

The National Clearinghouse for Alcohol and Drug Information www.health.org/index.htm is a national resource sponsored by the U.S. government. Searchable databases www.health.org/dbases.htm allow user to search papers on any topic related to alcohol use.

National Commission Against Drunk Driving (NCADD) www.ncadd.com This group continues efforts of the Presidential Commission on Drunk Driving by uniting public and private sector organizations.

National Substance Abuse Web Index http://nsawi.health.org Information on substance abuse prevention and treatment communities. Excellent links.

NIAAA -National Institute on Alcohol Abuse and Alcoholism. http://www.collegedrinkingprevention.gov/default.aspx Devoted to changing the college drinking culture with college policies, reports, research links.

Olson, Nancy. *With a Lot of Help from Our Friends: The Politics of Alcoholism.* Writers Club Press, 2003.

Outside the Classroom www.outsidetheclassroom.com Colleges and universities use this product, AlcoholEdu, as a prevention effort to negate consequences of alcohol abuse on campus.

Peterson, Vincent J., B. Nisenholz, G. Robinson. *A Nation Under the Influence: America's Addiction to Alcohol.* New York: Alyn & Bacon, 2003.

Sober Living in Delray. http://www.sober-living.com/base2.php?id1=home&id2=x Early sobriety halfway facility.

Students Against Destructive Decisions (SADD) www.saddonline.com prevention programs for middle school, senior high and college students for underage drinking, drug abuse, destructive decisions.

Task Force on College Drinking www.collegedrinkingprevention.gov Sponsored by the National Institute on Alcohol Abuse and Alcoholism (NIAAA), the site offers information about the alcohol problem on college campuses; possible solutions.

Wechsler, Henry, and Bernice Wuethrich. *Dying to Drink: Confronting Binge Drinking on College Campuses.* New York City: Rodale, 2002.

Appendix 1

The Twelve Steps of Alcoholics Anonymous

1. We admitted we were powerless over alcohol—that our lives had become unmanageable.

2. Came to believe that a Power greater than ourselves could restore us to sanity.

3. Made a decision to turn our will and our lives over to the care of God as we understood Him.

4. Made a searching and fearless moral inventory of ourselves.

5. Admitted to God, to ourselves and to another human being the exact nature of our wrongs.

6. Were entirely ready to have God remove all these defects of character.

7. Humbly asked Him to remove our shortcomings.

8. Made a list of all persons we had harmed, and became willing to make amends to them all.

9. Made direct amends to such people wherever possible, except when to do so would injure them or others.

10. Continued to take personal inventory and when we were wrong promptly admitted it.

11. Sought through prayer and meditation to improve our conscious contact with God as we understood Him, praying only for knowledge of His will for us and the power to carry that out.

12. Having had a spiritual awakening as the result of these steps, we tried to carry this message to alcoholics, and to practice these principles in all our affairs.

Source: Alcoholics Anonymous, 1985

Appendix II

The Short Michigan Alcohol Screening Test (SMAST)

1. Do you feel you are a normal drinker?
2. Does your wife, husband, a parent, or other near relative ever worry or complain about your drinking?
3. Do you ever feel guilty about your drinking?
4. Do friends or relatives think you are a normal drinker?
5. Are you able to stop drinking when you want to?
6. Have you ever attended a meeting of Alcoholics Anonymous (AA)?
7. Has your drinking ever created problems between you and your wife, husband or other near relative?
8. Have you ever gotten into trouble at work because of your drinking?
9. Have you ever neglected your obligations, your family, or your work for two days in a row because you were drinking?
10. Have you ever gone to anyone for help about your drinking?
11. Have you ever been in a hospital because of drinking?
12. Have you ever been arrested for drunken driving, driving while intoxicated, or under the influence of alcoholic beverages?
13. Have you ever been arrested, even for a few hours, because of other drunken behavior?

SCORING: Each question answered YES scores 1 point except for questions 10 & 11 which are 3 points for each YES answer.

✓ A score of one or less points indicates "Non-Alcoholic."
✓ A score of two points indicates "Possibly Alcoholic."
✓ A score of three points or more indicates "Alcoholic."

Source: www.bhcpns.org/TheFriary/ScreeningTest.aspx

Author CHRIS VOLKMANN, a former classroom teacher and recipient of the 2001 Washington State Artist Trust GAP Literary Grant, lives in Olympia, Washington. Chris stepped away from her career to parent three sons. Once thinking herself a successful mother, she now restirs the pot of family-binding glue.

Co-author TOREN VOLKMANN (BA in psychology, former Peace Corps Volunteer) grips the story with the bite of an addict's hidden desperation. His edgy writing wanders within itself, giving the reader the feeling of chaos and inner turmoil behind a demeanor of courage. Toren currently lives one day at a time in New York City after successfully completing six months residence in a Florida halfway house.

For further exploration of alcohol choices and the consequences of chronic heavy drinking, go to:

www.OurDrink.com

Invite Toren Volkmann and Chris Volkmann for honest talk about alcohol choices.

- ✓ Speaking services
- ✓ Available programs
- ✓ Workshops offered

Each program is tailored to individual needs and preferences.

NOTES